C5

C5

From Impact to Recovery

A Wife's Memoir

By

Judith Jo Pachino

Copyright @2018 by Judith Jo Pachino

Cover Design by Ella Edelman

ExhaleBooks Publishing
Baltimore, Maryland

First Edition: January 2018

ISBN 13: 978-0692966051
ISBN 10: 0692966056

Printed in the United States of America

Foreword

Reading this book, I got to relive one of the hardest chapters in my life. Mel and Judy have been our close friends for over 25 years. On the fateful day of his terrible accident I was paged to return to the hospital with limited information, just hearing that Mel was flown to Shock Trauma after a biking accident. I immediately went back into "Dr. Mode" knowing that I could help most translating and decision making. Over the next grueling months I went in and out of doctor and friend mode many times. I learned that friend and doctor can be the same thing.

In this remarkably accurate account, we get to know Judy as a medical novice who became an expert in all aspects of one patient. A tireless advocate for Mel, she had to learn how to balance his health, her sanity and the endless love of friends family and community. We see how Mel and Judy brought the best out of each other, learned to accept the kindness of friends, and brought a whole community together.

In this account, we see how their faith protected and nourished them while showing the uninitiated how deep communal concern uplifted them and their family. Although we see Mel's illness and recovery through Judy's Jewish religious eyes, the lessons that shine forth are universal.

People who have learned from Mel and Judy's transformative experience have shared with me that they are closer with their spouses. Nurses and other hospital workers have commented on how they now know why they went into their fields. They have also commented on how they never met a couple or a group of friends as dedicated and determined. Some have commented that they had never met a religious Jewish family and were deeply impressed with how they relate to their friends and caretakers.

For Mel and Judy's friends, all was done with love and caring. For their community, so many people stepped forward without question when asked. Community prayer, psalms readings, charity and acts of kindness were dedicated to his recovery.

I think this book is a "must read" for anyone going through injury, illness or personal tragedy. Judy shows how doctors, nurses, therapists and hospital workers are true heroes. It provides a framework for action for loved ones, friends and community and gives the reader a personal glimpse into how a loving couple helps heal in the face of overwhelming adversity, aided by those whom they hold dear.

Finally, we see how a kind, tough determined man, who dedicated his life to helping others, succeeds in triumphing over tragedy. We feel his pain, and rejoice in his triumph. His tenacity, faith and acceptance shine through via Judy's narrative.

Please enjoy reading her account and learn unique lessons, as I have.

Jack Gladstein, MD
Professor of Pediatrics and Neurology
University of Maryland School of Medicine
Mel and Judy's friend

Preface

On May 3, 2013, my husband, Mel, took a ride on his bicycle. Less than a mile from our home, he hit his stride as he approached the intersection of Smith Avenue and Carla Road. Coming up Smith Avenue from the opposite direction was a black SUV. Visibility was optimum on that temperate spring day, and the driver reported that he clearly saw the cyclist coming toward him. Grossly misjudging the speed Mel was traveling and the distance, the driver turned left, effectively cutting Mel off. Bike met car with enough force to send my husband and his bike into the air. The driver walked away from the collision. My husband did not.

In one moment, our lives were changed forever. The next months were the stuff of nightmares. I have learned that there is much in life that is out of our control. The only thing truly in our control is how we choose to handle what comes our way. My husband is an amazing role model for this. His story of faith and determination is one that we felt was worth sharing.

Acknowledgments

Thank you to my editor, Debbie Rapps, for her guidance, professionalism, generosity and love. Your talent for finding clarity in the written word made all the difference.

Thank you to our friends, our extended family. The memories expressed in the story are just a sampling of the genuine kindness you exemplify.

Thank you to my extraordinary daughters, sons-in-law and grandchildren for fueling my love and appreciation for the good in the world. You mean everything to me.

Thank you to Mel. You are the hero of my story and my life.

Dedication

To Mel's therapists and doctors, who rebuilt him with their skill, wisdom and dedication

To the Baltimore Jewish Community, who taught us the meaning of chesed

Glossary of Terms

Baalat Teshuva	One who has returned to the Faith
Baruch Hashem	Thank God
Beit Mikdash	Holy Temple
Bikur Cholim	Visiting the sick; organization name
Bracha	Blessing
Brachot	Blessings
Brit Milah	Circumcision
Chag samayach	Happy Holiday
Chesed	Acts of kindness
Daven	Pray
Dayenu	It would have been enough for us
Hakadosh Baruch Hu	God
Hakarat haTov	Gratitude for the good God showers
Hashem	God
Havruta	Study partners
Kehillah	Group
Minyanim	Prayer services with a quorum
Mitzvot	Good deeds
Motzei Shabbat	After the Sabbath
Nishama	Soul
Pesach	Passover
Saba	Grandfather
Savta	Grandmother

Shabbat	Sabbath
Shabbatot	Sabbaths
Shabbat Shalom	A peaceful Sabbath
Shiurim	Classes
Shul	Synagogue
Smachot	Joyous occasions
Tallit	Prayer shawl
Tefillin	Phylacteries
Yad Hashem	The hand of God
Yom Ha'aim Samayach	Happy Mother's Day

Prologue

MEL

May 3, 2013

"That's my grandson!" I exclaimed, smiling broadly. "Akiva's always on the move. Is he calling you?" I asked Shana as I heard a child babbling over the phone.

"Of course, I know, I know. It's almost time for Shabbat," I said, waving absently to my wife Judy, who was heading out to a yoga class. "Go to that wonderful son of yours. Let me just give you a bracha before we hang up."

As I brought my mouth closer to the phone and carefully recited the traditional pre-Shabbat blessing that a father gives a daughter, I smiled again and pictured our beautiful middle child. Although she lives 6000 miles away in Israel and has a family of her own, Shana was momentarily right there beside me – forever my little girl.

"Speak to you on Sunday. Yes. I'm going for a ride. It's a perfect day. You know it usually rains every time I get a chance to ride my bike. The sun is shining for a change," I laughed. "Miracles never cease, right Shana? Okay. Speak to you soon. Have a great Shabbat and give my grandson a kiss from his Saba."

I shut my cell and tried not to think about how much I miss my grandson as I tucked the phone into the back pocket of my neon yellow cycling shirt and tugged it down over my black riding shorts. Grabbing my helmet on the table by the door, I positioned it on my head and strapped it into place. With my left hand, I lifted my Specialized brand bicycle from the hallway wall, opened the door and carried the bike through the porch and down the five front steps to the street. After checking the air in the tires and scanning the sky, I decided the ride was a go.

I rode out of our small cul-de-sac down a short block to Smith Avenue, a residential two-lane road, and waited briefly for the traffic to pass and turned left onto Smith. Using my street sense, I rode close to the curb, just where a bike lane would be had there been one on Smith Avenue. The day really was perfect for a good workout, I thought as I hit my stride, my cadence smooth and fluid, my legs and heart pumping.

Riding along and feeling really good, I noticed a black sedan approaching from the opposite side of the road. I watched without concern.

Unexpectedly and without signaling, the sedan began to make a left turn, crossing the median and appearing directly in my path. Oh my God, I'm going to hit that car, I thought frantically as I realized I had nowhere to go and no way to avoid the impending crash. There was simply no time, no option. A silent yet earth-shattering *NO! NO! NO! NO!* repeated itself through my stunned mind the instant I crashed into the car and felt my body flying up up up and then over over over through the air, my bicycle left far behind. I landed with a terrible thud, face down on the roadway. My head snapped back with a sickening crack.

Day 1 – The Accident
JUDY

May 3, 2013

The funeral chapel was full. Mr. B's wife, children and grandchildren solemnly walked toward the front bench and sat down almost in unison. I looked to my right and briefly clasped hands with my best friend Pam. She nodded at me with compassionate brown eyes, and I knew we were both thinking about Mr. B, a kind and devoted member of our synagogue, a warm person always with a ready smile.

As I listened to the eulogies from the family members and then the rabbi of our synagogue, my mind naturally wandered to my own beloved family; my husband of almost 29 years, Mel, our grown daughters Rebecca, Shoshana and Yael, our sons-in-law Simcha and Moshe; our adorable, small grandchildren Shira, Eliora and Akiva. I pictured each precious face as Mr. B's life was described in review. I know and agree that funerals are depressing and sad. Yet through the haze of loss, I always find inspiration. I am truly amazed at the lives of others, what they have done, their achievements, the depths of love they have engendered. Each life story is unique. Each soul makes its impact.

My heart was heavy as I felt the loss of Mr. B's family. Much was said about Mr. B's work with the synagogue. I know that he worked on many synagogue committees through the years with Mel. We are about a generation younger and I know that Mel highly respected Mr. B's opinions. Mel loves charitable work. Among the various positions he has held at our synagogue, he has served at the layman's highest positions of president and vice president. Over the years, he has committed himself to at least a dozen organizations throughout Baltimore, attending the numerous meetings after his long days as a community pharmacist. His uncanny memory for names, faces and personal details makes him a natural people person and leader. I do not share such a formidable memory, but I do think we as a team truly care about our fellow man.

Pam and I stood for the concluding prayers and stepped closely together as the casket was pushed past our row. Silently we followed the other funeral attendees toward the side door of the chapel. We were swallowed by the crowd with our petite builds and dark hair. Reaching into our pocketbooks, we simultaneously pulled out sunglasses as we emerged from the building and headed to my car on that spring day.

Once home, I breezed through the house and passed Mel, who was sitting on the sofa in our living room. I knew that he was upset over having to miss the funeral for work. Although it was his day off, he had needed to finish up an audit at Rite Aid, where he worked as a pharmacist and pharmacy manager.

I wasn't home for long and needed to get ready for my yoga class. I rushed by him, and not noticing that he was on the phone, began to tell him about the funeral. When I realized that he was talking to our daughter Shana in Israel, I gave a quick see-you-later wave, and held back from my usual, "be careful when you ride" line. I ran to class and made it with just moments to spare. Life can be really hectic when you make it so.

***

I returned home after class and looked around for Mel, surprised that he wasn't chugging some water and dripping on the foyer floor. He's probably in the shower, I thought as I went upstairs. No shower running. Returning downstairs, I opened the front door and peered outside. No Mel. So, I decided to make an open-faced tuna melt in the toaster oven. While the tuna melt heated, I saw two police officers walking up my drive through our glass storm door. I thought back to earlier in the day and the bad feeling I had had about Mel's bike ride. I often had a bad feeling about his biking. With trepidation, I met the two officers, one man and one woman, coming up the walkway to our house.

"Are you Mrs. Pachino?" asked the male officer.

"Yes. What happened?"

"Your husband was in an accident. He's at Shock Trauma."

"Sinai?" I asked, feeling completely confused.

"No. He's at Shock Trauma. He's okay."

"What ... happened?"

"He was hit by a car as he passed the intersection of Smith Avenue and Carla Road. The driver failed to yield the right of way. He was at fault. We have your husband's bike. Should I take it around back?"

"No. I'll bring it inside," I said motioning to the front door.

"I'll do that for you," he offered.

As he rolled the bike past me and through the door, I noticed that it wasn't damaged. Hope flared briefly – very briefly. The female officer reached into the police cruiser, pulled something out and placed it in my hands. It was Mel's bloodied helmet.

"What's the blood from?" I asked looking into her downturned face, trying to reconcile hearing "he's okay," and seeing Mel's undamaged bike with the dried blood.

5

"We think he may have broken his nose," the male officer interjected, cutting off any response she may have had.

"Oh," I replied. "Where is Shock Trauma?" How had I managed to live fifty years in Baltimore and not know the exact location of such a well-known trauma hospital? Downtown - somewhere - was all I could muster.

"Are you going to follow her?" I heard the female officer say to her partner, but he didn't answer either of us.

The two officers edged toward the curb, leaving almost as suddenly as they had arrived. Surprised and confused, I watched them get into their vehicle and heard the engine start. I watched until their car turned right onto Wickfield and continued toward Willow Glen.

As their car disappeared from sight, I slowly and very hesitantly turned and walked inside the house, quietly closing the door behind me. Crazily, I remembered the tuna melt in the toaster oven and ran to turn it off, expecting to find it burnt to a crisp. But it hadn't burned. My interaction with the two police officers happened so fast − the few brief minutes it took for the cheese to melt between the slices. While placing the foil-laden tuna melt on the counter, I picked up the nearby phone.

Where do you turn at the first sign of trouble? In my case − to my soul sister and best friend Pam, whom I called after the abrupt departure of the two officers. I looked over at Mel's bike. It looked perfectly fine, which confused me. Hadn't the stocky, no-nonsense policeman told me that Mel was okay? But he also said that they took Mel to Shock Trauma. The policewoman handed me the bloody helmet still dangling from my left hand. No, the situation was not okay; and she somehow conveyed this more loudly than her meager explanation of Mel's broken nose. Unsure of where to place the offensive helmet, I wandered over to the bike and stroked the seat. Eventually, I hung the bloodied thing on the handlebars.

Walking up the stairs to our bedroom I dialed Pam's cell, not expecting her to answer. As a social worker in the Baltimore city school system her days were usually hectic. Relief flooded through me when she answered on the second ring.

The words came pouring out of me.

"Mel was hit by a car and is at Shock Trauma."

"I'll be there in fifteen minutes," Pam replied. Accustomed to emergencies and trained to react quickly she instructed me to take extra clothing for Mel along with some snacks. "You may be there awhile."

"That's a good idea," I said, relieved to have something concrete to do while I waited.

"I'll be there in fifteen minutes," she repeated reassuringly.

I sprinted upstairs and started to frantically search for things Mel might need. I grabbed a sweatshirt in case it was cold in the hospital.

I need to hear Becca's voice, I thought, even if I have to listen to it over a voicemail. As I dialed our oldest daughter's number, I tried formulating a message, since I didn't expect to reach her during her busy workday. Becca is an occupational therapist for the New Jersey school system and is usually with students and unable to take personal calls during work.

The stars were aligned it seemed, because she picked up just as Pam had earlier.

"Becca," I began, "Dad was hurt while riding his bike. I don't know much, but he was taken to Shock Trauma. Two policemen just came to the house. They said that Dad is okay, but didn't give me any details."

"Oh, Mom, should we come home?" Becca instinctively understood the gravity of the situation and wanted to be there for us.

"No, I don't think you should come yet," I said knowing how complicated it would be for her to run home, pack up, gather the kids from day care, get her husband Simcha from his Brooklyn office and drive to Baltimore – a three hour trip on a good day – all before the start of Shabbat. It just seemed impossible. It was already after noon.

"I'll let you know more when I get to the hospital. Pam is picking me up in about ten minutes. I'll call you as soon as I know more."

"Are you sure?"

"Not really," I conceded. "I don't know anything yet, but I'll keep you posted."

"We're coming, Mom. Take some money and the phone charger with you."

"I don't know that you need to come, but do whatever you think. I'm going to pack up the clothes and snacks Pam suggested I bring, plus the money and phone charger right now. I'll call you as soon as I know something. I love you."

"I love you too, Mom. I'll be waiting to hear."

I gathered the few items, grateful that I actually had some cash on hand, and headed back downstairs. Glancing at my cell, I realized I had missed a call. As usual, I had not turned the sound back on after my yoga class. While opening the front door to watch for Pam I listened to the voicemail. It was from the hospital. I quickly called the number.

"I'm not sure who I need to speak to, but my husband was taken to your hospital today."

"What's your husband's name?"

"Mel Pachino."

"Yes, Mrs. Pachino. I'm here with your husband now."

"You are? How is he?"

"He's doing fine. He's asking for you."

"Tell him I'm on my way. I should be there in about a half-hour."

"Take your time, Mrs. Pachino. We're taking care of him."

"Thank you. The policemen didn't give me details. Is he hurt?"

Without hesitation, she said, "We think he has a broken arm and a broken nose."

"Oh," I said, somewhat relieved. "Tell him I'm coming and that I'm bringing him extra clothes. Does he need anything else?"

"No. That will be fine. We'll see you soon."

Pam pulled her car into the driveway just as I was hanging up. She was instantly by my side with a hug and questioning eyes.

"I just spoke to Mel's nurse," I began, "She told me he has a broken nose and a broken arm. It doesn't sound so bad. When I saw the helmet, I began to panic."

"Do you have the food and clothes?" Pam asked.

"Yes," I said, lifting the small bag.

She checked that I had my pocketbook and ushered me out the door.

"You can fill me in on everything on the way," she said. "Let's go."

As Pam drove, I recounted every word from my phone calls. We were both relieved that Mel had such minor injuries and our mood lightened.

"You know," I said, "he is going to be really pissed about his arm."

"Yes he will," she agreed.

"And it's probably the sixth time he's broken his nose," I added.

We actually laughed at that, something that would make us shudder soon after. In "blissful" ignorance we made our way to the University of Maryland Medical Center on Greene Street, failing to allow the fact that we were heading to Shock Trauma to fully register.

The Locked Floor

Pam parked the car in an underground lot just a short half-block from the hospital. Our earlier bravado evaporated as soon as we entered the massive Medical Center. With hands intertwined, we approached the reception desk where the receptionist wrapped a pink paper hospital bracelet around each of our wrists.

"Pink must be the color for Shock Trauma," I said as we raced down the hallway going deeper and deeper into the bowels of the hospital. We stopped at the desk, and I asked the receptionist where I could find my husband. A nurse was dispatched, and she accompanied us to a secured floor. She guided us through what looked like an intensive care unit, where curtained treatment areas bordered the large space with nursing stations at various intervals. I noticed furtive glances as we passed. Suddenly our escort stopped and I felt Pam recoil. I peeked into the partially opened curtain to my right.

"That isn't Mel," she said referring to the bloodied man lying on the bed in the middle of the space.

"Yes, it is," I replied barely getting the words out. I felt her tug on my hand, pulling back. Recognizing her fear, I released her hand to give her the space she needed.

"I'll wait for you here," she whispered.

I entered the cubicle. A handsome young doctor in scrubs stepped forward and introduced himself as an acquaintance of Mel's. Generously, he offered his help in navigating the Shock Trauma system even though he was not officially assigned to Mel's case. Although I was not at all sure why we would need his help, I thanked him and continued toward Mel's bedside.

Gently, I touched Mel's cheek, which was caked with blood. Why hasn't anyone cleaned him up, I wondered.

"I'm here, honey."

"It wasn't my fault, I didn't do anything wrong," Mel insisted.

"Of course not. I'm sure you were careful."

"It wasn't my fault, it wasn't my fault," he said repeatedly.

"I know. I know. It's going to be okay," I said in my most reassuring voice though I wasn't sure of anything. A gaping hole now took the place of the front tooth that had been there hours before and blood covered most of his face. He was most likely in shock, judging by his level of agitation, but I had no information to go on. My attention was focused only on Mel. The world at that moment was just the two of us.

Suddenly I looked up, emerging from my own fog, surprised to see that the bed was surrounded by staff. A woman stood directly across from me, and I assumed she was Mel's nurse and possibly the person I spoke to over the phone. It seemed that the group was waiting for some signal from me. I tried to formulate questions, anything to shed light on what was happening, but I didn't know where to begin. Mel – a pharmacist by profession – is the medical one in our marriage. I always relied on him to help me understand all things health related. This was way out of my league.

Catching my eye the nurse explained that Mel needed to go for an MRI immediately. "We have to get him ready. The doctor will get your consent."

As if on cue, the room came to life and the staff began to do what was needed. I reached over and gave Mel a soft kiss on his forehead, afraid that someone would tell me that I was hurting him. Confused – and definitely still clueless – I was ushered out.

"I'll be waiting for you, I'll be here," I called out just before the curtain was drawn, separating us like a steel door. I felt no one would let me back in. We had had our moment. Mel might clinically be in shock, and I suppose I was too.

Dumbfounded, I turned to Pam who was speaking softly to the kind Dr. Ron, who I had met moments before. Pam pulled me in for a hug. She reached for my hand as Dr. Ron led us away. I had only been given a few precious minutes with Mel and I was still reeling. In those few minutes, I came to a harsh realization: We did indeed need Dr. Ron's assistance. Something was very wrong.

In just a few short moments, Dr. Ron would give that something a name:

SCI. Spinal Cord Injury.

One of the most devastating injuries to the human body.

With fingers interlaced, Pam and I followed Dr. Ron into the elevator and down to the first floor waiting room where he explained that Mel's cervical spine had been injured. An MRI was needed immediately to assess the extent of the injury so the team could develop a plan of action. Someone would be in shortly to get my signed consent, he gently added. His kindness, both then and for weeks to come, would become legendary. He became our guardian angel.

"I'll make myself available for anything you may need. I'll answer any questions you have," he offered.

Pam led me to a chair. We both sat down.

"It's really bad, isn't it?" I said, not really expecting an answer and not waiting for one either. "I need to call Becca back and I need to contact Yael."

Our youngest daughter was a student at the University of Maryland College Park. Although she didn't have a car at her disposal, I knew Yael would manage to get to me quickly. I wasn't surprised when the call went straight to voicemail. A true millennial, Yael's preferred method of communication was texting.

Yael, please call me ASAP, I texted.

The phone rang almost immediately.

"Hi honey," I said, relieved to hear Yael's voice. "Dad was in an accident. It's bad. I need you to come home."

"I have to work tonight," she replied, unaware of the extent of the accident.

"I need you to come home now."

I could almost see her face as she began to understand the situation. She knew I would never tell her to come home, unless it was a true emergency. Her response was rapid-fire. "I'll be there. Which hospital?" I filled in the details.

"Okay Mom, I'm on my way."

The waiting room began to get busy as I watched the scene unfold around me. Mel's brother Ronnie and many of our closest friends began to arrive. I know this could not have been easy for Ronnie, who was likely experiencing emotional déjà-vu. Just six months earlier he received the devastating news in this very waiting room that his oldest son was killed in a car accident. I watched him pace back and forth, fear and sadness written all over his face. Pam continued to text our friends. I signed the consent form and by that time Mel was already on his way to the MRI. Suddenly, a young woman stood in front of me with another consent form, this time to allow Mel to be part of a research study.

"We need him to remain in the MRI for an additional fifteen minutes," she explained.

Time was critical, the nurse emphatically told me just moments before when she took my consent forms. She explained that the MRI results were needed almost immediately so that the doctors could proceed as quickly as possible to minimize the injury. Dr. Ron summarily discounted my concerns and explained that those few extra minutes would not delay any treatment.

I signed another consent form.

The stack was growing.

Becca called to check in and to let me know that they were on their way. Relief flooded through me and I brushed away my previous concern about them reaching town before Shabbat. We needed them here.

Yael

At the time of the accident, our daughter, Yael was a student at the University of Maryland. She wrote an essay recording her experiences that fateful day. In her words:

As I'm mindlessly flipping through my Hebrew notes for my quiz in about thirty seconds, I feel my phone vibrate in my pocket. It's a text from my mom. "Call me ASAP." I reply automatically "Is something wrong?" As the teacher starts handing out the quiz, it's no longer my biggest concern. I feel my phone vibrate again, and although I shouldn't check it, I do. "No." My heart stops. I put my name on the quiz and hand it in without a second thought. As I fumble to grab my things, I see my hands are shaking. The girl next to me asks me if I'm okay. I give her a weak excuse for a smile and turn away.

I dial my mom as I'm fleeing from the classroom. No answer. A million terrible scenarios flash through my mind. I call her again as I rush down the stairs. No answer. Again. No answer. Finally she calls me back "Honey?" Her voice isn't as strong and sure as usual. I feel my eyes tearing up. Is it my sister? My grandmother? My cousin? "Mom, just say it." I'm pacing back and forth right outside of Susquehanna Hall. I feel the sun beaming down on me, I hear the birds chirping above me, and I feel a lump forming inside of me "Daddy was in an accident; it's really bad sweetie, You have to come here now. We're in Shock Trauma."

My dad? My dad is never hurt. Never scared. Always strong.

"How bad is it?" I say as I lean against the wall for support. I hear my mom sigh.

"I'm not so sure honey. Just come here. I need you. I'm scared."

I hang up the phone. I can barely breathe. I must be dreaming. I have to be dreaming. I call my friend Martin and within an hour we are speeding down 95 to the University of Maryland Shock Trauma in downtown Baltimore. I don't say a word. Martin doesn't seem to mind. He puts his hand on mine. All I can think about is how horrible I've been. I haven't spoken to my Dad in months. We've had our differences about religion and life choices. Last week he sent me an email saying how he wished we'd work through our problems. I didn't reply. I told myself I'd reply when I was less busy, but honestly, I had no intention of responding. Too many things were said, too many feelings were hurt. Now, we might never have the chance to say anything. I might not have the chance to say goodbye.

I grab my things from the backseat of Martin's car.

"Everything will be okay," he calls out. I thank him for the ride and run inside.

I've never been to the University of Maryland Hospital. I look lost and confused and realize that most of the people in here are probably just as lost and confused as I am. A woman smiles at me from behind the welcome desk and asks me if I know where I'm going.

"Um, I'm looking for Shock Trauma."

She gives me directions and slaps a pink wrist band on me. I mumble thank you and walk away. As I turn the corner, I see familiar faces: the rabbi of our congregation, my mom's best friend, my dad's brother.

This can't be happening.

No one says a word, but my uncle points to a small waiting room at the end of the hall. It feels like it's a million miles away. I rush past them and finally see my mom. As our eyes meet I can't hold back the tears any longer. She's just standing there, looking small, scared and alone. Somehow, as if by magic, my legs move toward my mom and I'm finally within reach.

She grabs on to me. Everyone else leaves the waiting room.

"He's a good man, he's a good man," my mom says as her tears fall down the back of my shirt. I stroke her hair. I whisper words of encouragement and force myself to stop crying because now I must be strong. Now my mom needs me in a way I wish she didn't.

Eventually I get my mom to stop shaking and sit down. As if on cue, the familiar faces return to the waiting room. My mom won't let go of my hand. She clutches onto me as if I'm her last hope. People race around us. Doctors come in and explain that my dad will need to have two spine surgeries within the next 24 hours. They don't know if he is going to be able to walk again. They don't know if he is going to make it.

I realize that I still don't know how my dad ended up here. How I went from sitting in a college classroom to sitting in a Shock Trauma waiting room. As if she can read my mind, my mom explains that my dad was riding his bike and was hit by a car. The driver thought he could beat my dad, but instead he hit him and sent him flying.

A young doctor leads my mom and me upstairs to see my dad. There are wires and machines everywhere. The only part of his body I can see is his face, swollen and bruised, his lip busted, two front teeth chipped, his eyes are disoriented and lost.

As they begin to wheel him out of the room my dad makes them stop in front of mom and mouths, "I was being safe, it wasn't my fault," and then he's gone. My mom and I stand there for a few more minutes.

She holds on to me and repeats, "He's a good man Yael; he's such a good man."

Surgery 1

The wait was in full swing when I looked up and saw Yael coming through the waiting room door. She had managed the trip in just over an hour. I was up from my seat and halfway to her before I even realized I had moved. With tears stinging my eyes, I fell into her arms, nearly knocking her to the floor.

Shortly thereafter, three doctors arrived and ushered the group out of the room, leaving Yael and me huddled together on a small sofa and my brother-in-law standing by the door. They arranged a few chairs in the center of the room and sat three across facing us. The one closest to me was the spokesman. Dr. P. introduced himself and his colleagues and proceeded to explain.

"We reviewed your husband's MRI. He has an injury to his cervical spine at C5. The disk has been pushed to the side, but we are hoping that it may move back into position. We need to stabilize his neck to prevent further injury and he needs surgery to fuse the vertebrae from the front. We will need to fuse from C4-C7, above and below the point of injury. I'll be performing the surgery."

Straining forward rigidly, I listened with my whole being, hearing the words, understanding most but could only formulate one question. "When will you do the surgery?"

"We'll start as soon as possible to reduce any further trauma. The surgery will take about eight hours. We need your consent," he said as he handed me another consent form and a pen.

"I understand," I said as I read over and signed the consent form, the many possible risks clearly delineated. "Please take care of him," I added, shaking.

"We will. He may need a second surgery to stabilize the back of his neck as well. We don't think that will be necessary at this point, but I'll be back after the surgery to speak to you."

As soon as they left Dr. Ron came into the room. "Did you understand what they told you?" he asked.

"I think so," I replied, proceeding to repeat what I had heard.

Satisfied, he asked, "Do you want to see Mel before he goes for surgery?"

I nodded and he led us out. A small crowd of our closest friends had gathered outside the waiting room door. Everyone was subdued, and the newcomers gave us quick hugs as we passed.

Once again by Mel's bedside, I tried to reassure him.

"Everything is going to be okay. We'll be right here waiting for you," I said, motioning Yael closer. "We'll see you after the surgery."

I kissed his forehead, which was still caked with blood. He asked no questions, and I offered no answers. There was simply too much, yet nothing to say.

***

The day was starting to wane. Mel was in surgery. Shabbat was coming. Everyone left except for Pam, Yael and me. Our community is truly incredible, a fact that I have come to know intimately. Through the remarkable work of the charitable organization *Bikur Cholim* and its dedicated volunteers, a refrigerator was brought to the hospital and set up in Mel's future hospital room. Kosher food was delivered to us, enough to feed at least ten people. Pam quickly got to work setting up the food in the refrigerator and separated some for us to use in the short term as we sat in the fourth floor waiting area by the Spinal Cord injury unit. With a tearful goodbye and repeated hugs, she went home to be with her family for Shabbat. She placed Yael's hand in mine and left.

A few minutes later, two little girls, one brown haired, one blond, burst through the waiting room door and jumped into my arms. Hugging my granddaughters tight to my heart, I smiled for the first time since arriving at the hospital. Becca had arrived with her husband Simcha and their two adorable daughters, Shira and Eliora.

"The traffic was terrible," Becca said, giving me a big hug and then turned to Yael. "It took us forever to get here."

"How's Dad?" Simcha asked.

"He's in surgery. It's supposed to take about eight hours," I related. "He should be in his room around 3 a.m."

"Oh," Becca said slumping into the nearest chair. They had raced all day in the hopes of making it to the hospital in time to see Mel before the surgery. A deep frown furrowing her brow, Becca said sadly, "We can't stay long, but we'll be back right after Shabbat."

As traditional Jews, we adhere to Orthodox guidelines for our religious practice. Shabbat begins at a predetermined time each week, calculated by the setting of the sun. Even though it was spring and sunset was nearly at its latest of the year, there was no squeaking out a few extra minutes to be with us. They still needed to get to our home some twenty minutes away before sundown when traditionally we can no longer drive. I could tell that Becca had struggled with the decision of whether to stay with us at the hospital or to be with her husband and children.

"Should I stay with you?" she asked.

21

I looked at her growing belly, seven months along in her pregnancy and saw the worry in her hazel eyes. I knew she was conflicted, and I also knew that she and Simcha had debated this most of the way to the hospital.

One word from me and Becca would have stayed, yet I wasn't sure that she should stay for an extended time in the hospital in her pregnant state. Also, I could not be the one to keep her from her family.

"Should I stay with you?" she asked again.

"You do what you need to do, honey. We understand. Yael will be here with me," I said.

After a brief but tremendously helpful visit, Becca and family left the hospital and made their way to our home for Shabbat. Another restricted activity during Shabbat is phone use. I knew that waiting the 25 hours of Shabbat, which begins an hour before sunset on Friday and ends at nightfall Saturday, would seem endless until they could find out how Mel was doing. Fortunately, we were able to alleviate a portion of that worry by sending word home with our friend Jack, a doctor in the hospital. Even so, it was an extremely anxious and difficult Shabbat for everyone.

Passing Becca and family in the hallway, my sister-in-law Shelley and niece Michelle came into the waiting area. With Yael by my side, we brought them up to speed on the developments. My brother Harry was out of town and couldn't make it. They would be regular visitors in the coming weeks.

The time for Shabbat arrived. It is customary to signal the start of Shabbat by lighting candles. Of course in a hospital, candles are not allowed. Our rabbi, who was one of the close group that met us outside the doors of the waiting room earlier, instructed me on how to deal with this unusual situation.

"I am about to begin Shabbat," I announced to my small group. Then I walked to the light switch and turned it off. Immediately I turned it back on. I had performed "the act of lighting." For the first time in over 28 years of marriage, I did not light Shabbat candles or say the blessing over the candles. I did not feel the ease of Shabbat enter my soul. So began the first of many extremely challenging *Shabbatot* for us.

Shelley and Michelle visited for a good while keeping us occupied. When they left, Yael and I turned to the food that was set up for us. We ate a bit. We waited. Eventually, we moved to Mel's future hospital room where the very kind nurses set up two fold-down chairs adjacent to our stocked refrigerator. It was in Room Number 8 where we set up house. We talked for hours; rest not being a viable option. Around midnight, I had a thought.

"What about his contacts?" I asked the nurse who checked on us.

She looked in his chart. "It doesn't say he had contacts on when he was brought in," she replied. "Are you sure he was wearing contacts?"

"Yes. He always wore his contacts and definitely when he rode his bike."

"I'll check with the surgical staff and get back to you."

My question was not as random as it seemed, because later the same nurse returned. She informed me that the surgical team had not removed his contacts prior to the first surgery, but they would be sure to do so before the second if need be.

Right on schedule, around 3 a.m., Mel was wheeled into the room.

"The surgery was a success," Dr. P. informed us. "But he will need a second surgery in the morning. The neck needs a good deal of support from the back, so his head won't eventually drop forward. The support will span from C4-T1," he explained.

Drop forward, I thought. Oh my God! Shaking my head, I asked, "Are you doing that surgery as well?"

"No. Dr. N. will lead that team."

Thanking the doctor, I turned my attention towards Mel's sleeping/post-surgery resting. He looked relatively comfortable. With him in the room, I was able to let go enough to sleep for a short while. Yael followed my lead. Jack was there when we woke up.

Surgery 2

Day 2

Jack is our dear friend and a remarkable pediatrician. A more humble, unassuming person you will never meet. He quickly became indispensable to me, virtually holding my hand during those first few weeks. Always calm and unflappable, Jack managed to find time in his extremely busy schedule as director of a prestigious clinic at the University of Maryland and associate professor to avail himself to me and my family at a moment's notice. I don't know how he did it; he just did. He stood by our side each day during the first two weeks of rounds, watching and explaining complicated medical jargon, repeating it patiently when I failed to understand or retain the information. A lesser person may have given up in frustration, but not Jack. He did such a wonderful job tutoring me that Mel's primary neurology resident believed I was a medical professional and spoke to me as a peer.

I awoke the first morning and found Jack, slight of build and impeccably dressed, checking on Mel. He had already finished his rounds. Glad to see him, I stiffly unfolded myself from the chair and made my way to Mel's bedside with Yael close behind me. The three of us watched Mel for a few minutes.

"The surgery went well," Jack said.

"Yes, thank God", I replied. "I think they are taking him for the second surgery around 10. They need to build up the support on the back of his neck."

"That's right," he nodded. "I want to show you something," he said, turning and heading to the hallway. "Follow me."

Jack took us down a stairway and around a few bends until we stopped at an open and airy waiting room filled with carefully arranged sofas, chairs and small tables. The high glass ceiling gave an outdoor feel to the large indoor space.

"This will be a nice place for you to wait today," Jack said. Yael and I agreed as we looked around the sun–drenched room, which was filled with comforting heat and light.

"Do you need anything?" Jack asked as we backtracked to the room.

"I don't think so. We have plenty of food for sure, thanks to *Bikur Cholim*. Are you headed home?"

"Yes. I'll spread the word that the first surgery was successful, and I'll see you first thing tomorrow."

By mid-morning, Mel was back in surgery and Yael and I returned to our vigil. The waiting room was rather empty that Saturday morning since only the most critical surgeries are performed on the weekend. We had our choice of spots, so we meandered around and finally plopped down on one of the sofas, settling in for the duration. When it got too hot, we returned to Mel's room to pick at some lunch. The day wore on and on. We headed back to the waiting room.

It was during the early afternoon that we decided it was time to call Shana. Although using the phone is prohibited on Shabbat, our rabbi felt the situation was critical enough to break the rules; it was necessary that I speak to our middle daughter as soon as Shabbat ended in Israel. Given the seven hour time difference, it was already nightfall there as I picked up the phone. Yael and I carefully rehearsed what I would say to break the news that Mel was severely injured and in surgery. With my heart in my throat I dialed the number. Voicemail. I left her a message to call me. I dialed again. Voicemail again. I tried again and again, panicking as the minutes ticked by and realizing that my chances of breaking the news to her myself were dwindling. Mel's accident had been reported on local television. The Baltimore community was very connected. Someone could have easily emailed or contacted someone she knew. Finally, on my umpteenth try, I saw her number pop up. She was calling me. "Mom," she said hearing my voice. "I already know."

"I'm so sorry honey, I wanted to be the one to tell you."

"It's okay. How is he?"

"I tried to call you the minute I thought you could pick up."

"My cell was off. Aryeh heard from his parents in Baltimore that something had happened right before he started Shabbat. He got a hold of Eitan, who was at our house, to find out if he knew anything. Eitan told Moshe and then Moshe told me. When I heard your message, we checked with our rabbi to make sure it was permissible to call you right back."

"You were calling me while I was calling you. Does anyone in the family know?" I asked, referring to Mel's sister and family also living in Israel.

"Yeah. They all know. Ari just called us. I'm not sure how the word got around so quickly. How is Abba?"

"He's in surgery now, his second operation. The first was successful and they stabilized his neck."

"Who's with you?"

"Yael is. She's been a rock. I don't know what I would have done without her. Becca is back at the house. She and

27

Simcha will be here right after Shabbat." Looking at Yael, I continued, "We are hanging in. Are you okay?"

"I'm fine. Moshe is here with me. Call me later. Let me know how the surgery went."

"Sure. Of course," I said.

"I'm going to go now Mom. We shouldn't stay on the phone," she said, referring to my using the phone on Shabbat.

"Rabbi S. said it was okay." Not wanting to hang up, I waited a few long moments and then conceded. "All right. I'll call you later. I love you."

"I love you too, Mom. I'll be waiting."

As the connection broke, my heart broke a little as well. "You did good," Yael said giving me a hug. "She's fine. You'll speak to her again soon."

About an hour passed. Mel's doctor found us sprawled on our sofa gazing at the sky high above.

"I'm Dr. N.," he said, pulling a chair toward us and sitting down. Distinguished good looks, mussed gray hair, seasoned eyes and a warm smile: Dr. N. exuded confidence.

"Your husband did very well. The second surgery went beautifully."

I felt my body ease a bit as I heard his reassuring words. He continued, "His neck is fully fixed now, fused in the front, supported in the back. He should have no further worries from it."

"Oh my – that's wonderful news!" I cried as Yael gave my hand a squeeze. Dr. N. explained that he only worked weekends at this point in his career, and that he had performed hundreds of similar operations. He was very optimistic, and this lightened our mood. Thanking him, we shook hands and he left. Yael and I immediately grabbed our few things and returned to Room 8. Mel was brought in just as we arrived. He was fairly alert.

"You did great, Mel. The doctor just told us that you shouldn't have any more problems from your neck. It's all fixed," I began. "Yael has been with me every minute. She's been wonderful," I said pulling her close. "You don't need any more surgeries," I said excitedly.

I knew he understood, because I saw it in his eyes just before he dozed off.

***

The staff at Shock Trauma was superb. The caring, sensitivity and commitment to excellent healthcare were evident in everything they did. Mel's first daytime nurse, Karen, seemed to take special interest in me, and she became my go-to nurse – the one I sought out for answers and extra support. As the day waned, Nurse Karen took me aside just outside Mel's room.

"You mustn't stay here tonight," she said noticing my fatigue. "We will take care of your husband. This is a marathon, not a sprint," she said with certainty, words I would hear repeatedly in the coming weeks. "You need to pace yourself. You need to take care of yourself if you are to be of any help to your husband. He needs you, so you must go home and get some sleep in your own bed."

"How can I leave him?" I asked.

"We'll take care of him. That's what we do here," she repeated. "You must get some sleep and get away for a short while. Come back first thing in the morning."

Reluctantly I agreed, admitting to myself that I was completely worn out.

"Will you be here tonight?" I asked.

"No, but Trisha will be his nurse again. She's excellent."

I had watched Trisha handle and care for Mel the previous

night. With compassion and professionalism, she had taken care of all his needs. She followed through on the contact situation and had gone above and beyond by ensuring not only Mel's comfort, but Yael's and mine as well. If I was to actually go home, then I was relatively comfortable leaving Mel in her capable hands. It still felt wrong, but I understood that Karen was right.

"Trisha was wonderful with all of us last night," I said, tacitly agreeing to go home.

"You're doing the right thing," she said as she turned down the hall.

The sun set on Day Two, signaling the end of Shabbat. It seemed like only moments before Becca and Simcha arrived, relieved to find that both surgeries had been successful. Together we gathered around Mel's bed and noticed a wondrous thing; Mel was still very much with us, his brain fully intact, still our beloved husband and father. He was alert and remarkably cheerful, and we enjoyed a wonderful visit with him, even though he was intubated and couldn't talk. His clear blue eyes spoke volumes. When he got tired, the kids urged me toward the door. I stood in the doorway looking at Mel for several long moments, wringing my hands, hesitant to leave.

I'm someone who follows the rules; I take direction extremely well. This is a trait that often causes me some friendly ridicule. I could still hear Karen's directive. Her words gave me the strength to move.

The exhausting day was finally over. I went home to sleep in our bed, alone. Taking the extra car, Yael headed back to school; the poor thing had finals the following week. Injuries and illnesses do not accommodate our personal schedules.

I slept only moments before the sound and sight of my granddaughters woke me. I pulled myself up and out of bed to begin a new, frightening day. I made pancakes for the family and cleaned up the kitchen, trying to feel a sense of normalcy. Then I headed to the hospital.

Once I arrived, I virtually kicked myself for dawdling when I realized I had missed rounds. What was I thinking? What was I doing? Nothing is normal. It's time to get with the program. Mel is the only priority, I admonished myself.

Day 3

The first full day of healing begins.

Becca and Simcha spent most of the morning visiting Mel in his room as we took turns playing with the girls in the waiting area. Children inspire hope; they remind us that there is a future, even during the most difficult of times. The time spent with Shira and Eliora gave me strength and optimism, and I know that Becca and Simcha's presence did the same for Mel. Needing to return to their jobs and the routine of everyday life, they left by mid-day. We understood. The parting was difficult, yet they made every effort to return as often as possible. Throughout the long months of recovery, Becca and Simcha made frequent trips to be with us. Each visit gave us a new jolt of life.

Most of our close friends who came to the hospital on Friday reappeared by Sunday afternoon. They helped me arrange what I would refer to as my office; the back portion of Mel's newly renovated room. With more than sufficient space, I had a refrigerator, table, multiple chairs, and electric outlets to conduct the business of getting Mel's life in order while the doctors and nurses got his health in order. From behind his hospital bed, I received assurance from Mel's manager at Rite Aid that his job would be held for him, no matter how long his recovery took; received confirmation of his insurance status; and communicated with family, friends and community members on his behalf.

Our friends congregated daily to review Mel's progress and offer suggestions, comfort, support and encouragement. It was on this first day as we assembled, speaking in low tones, that I told them about the CaringBridge website. Earlier in the day, Nurse Karen had recommended I set up an account for Mel and begin to write about his progress. She said it would be a great way to "get the word out" to many people at once, freeing me from repeated phone calls. I mentioned it to our friend, Gary, who is a real take-action kind of guy. Within minutes, he had confiscated my iPad and set up an account.

"Everybody loves Mel. People will want to know how he's doing. Use the site," he directed as he handed me the iPad. I took it hesitantly. What would I write? I thought. I guess I'll ask people to pray for Mel. And so it began. I wrote the first blog entry that day.

May 5, 2013

Mel's operations were very successful and his recovery has begun. We have a long road ahead but are very optimistic!

Our deepest appreciation to everyone for their prayers, concern and amazing chesed! We are deeply grateful and touched by the outpouring of love. Please continue to pray for Mel. These are critical days!

The first entry was short and heartfelt, its message, one of gratitude and a plea for prayer. The feedback was immediate, and I was surprised to find that quite a few people responded in the 'Reply' section. I read the encouraging messages to Mel.

Then I wrote again. Messages flooded back. Mel was buoyed by all the kind words; we knew we were not alone. Committing myself to the task, I made writing an important part of each day. Instinctively, I focused on writing about the positives, which helped to reinforce the positives for Mel and me. And then a truly awe-inspiring thing happened. The positivity I sent out through my posts was returned to us exponentially through positive energy in the form of messages, community action, and I believe, Heavenly reaction. The blog was fairly popular, and numerous people mentioned reading it daily and finding strength in their own lives from Mel's determination and faith. To this day, I am constantly amazed when community members share with me the impact the blog had on them personally. Firsthand, I experienced and learned the power of the written word.

Day 4 – Assessment

May 7, 2013
We are seeing forward progress. Please continue to daven and learn on Mel's behalf.

I rose early to face the new day, the new challenges. Following the GPS directions on my phone, I drove my green Honda CRV to Shock Trauma, determined that there would be no repeat of the previous day when I had missed rounds. Jack had made it his business to be there and I was eternally grateful. He had been able to fill me in, but I needed to be there in person. I could not allow that to happen again. I needed to ask questions and get answers for Mel. Information was essential, understanding the entire situation imperative. Mel was counting on me.

I parked in the underground lot closest to the hospital and made my way to the entrance and then to the quickly moving visitor entrance line. "Mel Pachino," I said to the hospital receptionist when it was my turn.

Mel's name popped up on the computer. "Shock Trauma," the receptionist stated choosing another neon pink paper bracelet and fastening it to my outstretched arm. Two days, and I already knew the drill. I also knew the way. My black Dansko clogs thumped along as I hastily traversed the incredibly long hallways, remembering to turn right at the entry level restrooms. The hospital was already bustling at 8:05 a.m., as I weaved my way to what I believed to be the farthest corner of the massive building. Finally, I reached the Shock Trauma elevators. Pressing the button for level four, I valiantly managed a small smile for the woman already in the elevator, as I moved toward the back wall.

Level four. I walked a few steps and pressed the button on the wall, the one that notified the unit that someone wanted to enter. I waited. Two more people joined me, each one furtively looking my way and pressing the button on their approach. With a swoosh, the doors swung open and I entered, turned left and made my way down another long hallway. I could not help noticing the patients as I passed. All the hospital beds faced the hallway. Palpable sadness and pain surrounded me, increasing my anxiety and urging me to increase my pace. Finally I arrived. The curtains were open and I could see him. "Mel, I'm here," I said with relief as I approached his bedside. "How are you today? How was your night?" I asked reaching for his hand while dropping my pocketbook into the chair by the bed. Unconsciously, I brushed my fingers gently along his listless hand. It would be weeks before Mel quietly told me that even though my touch had been gentle and he knew I was comforting him, my caress had actually been quite painful for him. I wince whenever I remember that I was causing him pain in my feeble attempt to comfort him.

He moved his head slightly; his intubation tube made answering by mouth impossible and the massive neck collar hindered movement. I took the nod to mean he was doing okay. We need to figure out a better way to communicate, I thought, not for the first time.

My phone buzzed, signaling a new text message. Reaching back, I picked up my pocketbook and fumbled around for my phone. Dropping the pocketbook back on the chair, I recognized that the text was from Jack reminding me to text him back as soon as I saw the doctors' teams approach for the morning rounds. There were two teams assigned to

Mel: the surgical team and the medical team. Jack had assured me that he wanted to be with us during rounds to help us understand the proceedings and the findings. Preparing the text response, I hurriedly typed, "They are here" without sending it and placed the phone on top of my pocketbook, where it was within reach.

"Honey, Jack wants to be here for rounds. I told him that would be wonderful. I'm so grateful for the help. I hope you don't mind. I want to understand everything that's happening," I told Mel.

Just then, Mel's day nurse came in and checked the monitor above Mel's head. "I'm Betsy," she said to me. "I'll be Mel's nurse today."

"Oh," I said, "is Karen off?"

"No, Karen's down the hall. She doesn't have Mel today."

Karen had been wonderful the first two days, and I was disappointed. "Do you often switch around?"

"We have new assignments every day. We aren't usually given the same patients day after day," she answered.

I was certainly not thrilled with that idea. Karen had been very solicitous of our little group; she had gotten Mel through the first terrifying days; she made sure that Yael and I had chairs that converted to loungers that first night for resting and sleeping, she had spoken kindly and helped me to begin to understand the gravity of our situation. She had even told me in no uncertain terms that I must go home at night, to maintain my health and keep my strength up. She was the first to say to me, "This is not a sprint; it's a marathon."

"How did Mel do last night?" I asked swallowing my disappointment.

"He did very well. Trisha said he got some rest."

"Oh, that's good," I replied turning toward Mel. "Honey, I'm really glad you were able to rest," I said. Trisha had been assigned to Mel the first two nights as well. What is going to happen tonight? I wondered.

"I'll also take good care of Mel," Betsy said. "Don't worry."

"Thank you," I replied distractedly as I got my first glimpse of the doctors' team coming down the hallway. Returning to the chair by Mel's bed, I retrieved my phone and punched SEND, hoping I had given Jack enough time to get here before the doctors. They were already at the patient next door.

I needn't have worried, because Jack was with us in minutes, way before the doctors' team. He greeted us both.

"How did you get here so fast?" I asked. "He had a good night."

"Great. My office is nearby. When I got your text, I was able to shift things around and leave right away."

Turning to Mel, Jack asked, "Mel, how are you, my friend? You look a bit tired but better than yesterday."

"Today, the team will be testing to see if the pathways are open throughout Mel's body," Jack told Mel and me. "The nervous system has been jumbled up by the spinal cord injury and the muscles have lost connection to the source. The body has the amazing ability to find and connect new pathways. They're going to see how things are coming along."

"Will it be painful – the testing?" I asked.

"No. I think Mel will be fine. Oh good, here comes the team," Jack said motioning toward the corridor.

A group of six doctors and residents approached Mel's bed, name tags dangling. They had already been briefed on Mel's accident, his surgeries and his current condition. One doctor stepped a bit closer and announced, "I am Dr. A. We are going to do an assessment this morning, Mr. Pachino. We will test your responses to pinpricks and then to cotton swabs."

"I am Dr. G.," Jack said to the doctors. "I'm here as a friend of the Pachinos."

"Very good," replied Dr. A. as he walked closer to Mel.

Nervously, I moved to the side of the room next to Jack, who also moved out of the way as the team of doctors surrounded Mel's bed.

"I understand you can move your left arm a bit. Is that true?" Dr. A. asked Mel.

Mel nodded.

"Good, that will be our signal. Here is the simple small pin we will be using to test," he said, showing Mel a small safety pin. "Please let us know when you feel the pin prick."

Mel nodded again in response. I could tell that he was exhausted from the simple interaction with Jack and me, but he forced himself to stay focused on the task at hand.

Dr A. began the testing at Mel's head and then over to the left shoulder and Mel immediately moved his left arm in response. As the testing continued, Mel's responses were a mixed bag. I could see that some areas were good, while others were not so good, but I couldn't find a pattern. My anxiety increased, but Jack calmed me with assurances that everything was going well. "Judy," he whispered, the sacral area is coming up soon. That's the area that controls the bowel, bladder and sexual function."

My focus had been on survival, movement of arms and legs, possible paralysis. I hadn't spared a thought to the most basic of human functions. I found it hard to breathe as a cold chill moved down my spine. Unable to look, I huddled behind Jack with my eyes tightly closed. "Please God," I prayed over and over, my lips moving silently, my ears shutting out the scene in front of me.

Moments later, I unglued my eyelids and snuck a tiny peek at Jack. Tears immediately flowed when I saw his thumbs up in response to my unasked question. Sucking in a long overdue breath, I watched with emotions roiling as Mel responded to the pin prick on his left foot but not to the prick on his right foot.

Jack moved closer and put his arm around me. "He did great," he whispered. "The pathways are open all around his body. This is very good."

The doctor repeated the entire sequence with the soft cotton Q-tip. Some yesses and some nos. My head was spinning by the time the assessment was completed. Mel didn't even look up when it was done. He fell asleep as soon as Dr. A. moved away.

"We will repeat the assessment in a few days," Dr. A. told us.

"Thank you doctor," I somehow choked out.

***

Near the end of the day, Karen stopped by Mel's room to speak to me. Motioning me to the side counter, she spent a minute clicking on the computer keys. I waited patiently not sure where this little meeting was heading. Raising her gaze to mine, she said, "Your husband's injury is very serious."

I nodded. That much I had figured.

"Everything below the point of injury is affected," she continued. Directing my attention to the computer screen, I had my first look at a dermatome, a diagram of the human body which shows the correlation between the vertebrae of the spinal cord and the parts of the body controlled by each area of the spinal cord.

I looked over the diagram, unsure. "But it's his neck," I blurted out.

"Yes, exactly," she replied looking directly into my eyes.

"Oh," I said, heart thumping. Turning my attention back to the monitor, I started from the neck area associated with C5 and scanned down the image noticing that both arms, torso, both legs were all controlled from below the point of injury.

"Will he be able to move at all?" I asked quietly.

"He should be able to breathe and to eat," she replied. "For everything else, we will need to wait and see." She patted me on the shoulder and as she walked away she said, "I'm around if you have any questions or need anything."

Stunned, but realizing that this was now my new normal, I spent a few more minutes studying the diagram. I walked slowly back to Mel's bedside. Everything below the point of injury, I winced. The day had started with optimism as Jack and I watched the pin and swab evaluation. "All the pathways are open," Jack had said. I held on to that thought. The pathways are open and everything is still possible. I sent one of a million heartfelt prayers toward Heaven. "Please God, please help him."

Intubation Extubation Intubation

Just before Mel was taken into his first surgery, the doctors inserted a breathing tube to help with his breathing. Once he went under general anesthesia, his diaphragm would be paralyzed and a ventilator was necessary to help him breathe. He continued to be intubated during the second surgery and for several days after. On the fourth day post surgeries, the doctors began to talk about extubation, the process of removing the tube. He was gaining strength; his oxygen saturation levels (sats) were looking good. The levels on Mel's ventilator were adjusted accordingly and the weaning process seemed to be progressing well.

Anticipation was building. This was the day that Mel would be extubated. The day looked bright and promising. The nurses were abuzz and around noon the final decision was made. It was a go.

As they readied Mel for the procedure, I was ushered out of the room and into the smaller of two waiting rooms at the end of the hallway. The social worker assigned to our case handed me papers and began to discuss discharge. I was incredulous; Mel could barely move! Things seemed to be traveling at warp speed. I listened as he outlined our options for the next phase of recovery, inpatient therapy. He described the two local hospitals with special spinal cord injury units and encouraged me to set up appointments to visit them immediately.

He walked me back to Mel's room just as the procedure was about to begin. Everyone was ready. I caught Mel's eye, and we both were nervous but excited. Standing by his side, I watched with eager anticipation as the tube was slowly pulled out. A few seconds ticked by... Mel's expression went from excitement to disbelief to anguish in quick succession. The look in his eyes defined terror, the rawness of it something I had never truly seen before. I almost collapsed on the spot. As curtains were drawn around Mel's bed, I was literally pulled from the room by one of the staff. We could hear frantic movement as the doctors and nurses worked on Mel.

Choking on my sobs, I asked, "What happened?"

The commotion had drawn a crowd in our portion of the hallway. I was guided to a chair.

"His lungs aren't able to work properly," someone answered.

"What's going to happen now? Is he going to die?" I asked.

"They will re-intubate him. They are doing it now," a voice behind me responded.

I was inconsolable. This was the first time since the incredible mess began that I had cried in public. I didn't know that it was possible for the extubation to fail. Even Karen had been confident that Mel would be able to breathe. One of the residents from Mel's A team stepped forward. Interestingly, my first impression of her had been less than favorable as I observed her stoic, cold expression during assessments. Yet she was the one to come forward while the others held back. She knelt down beside me and looked me right in the eye.

"He's going to be okay," she assured me. Our eyes stayed locked for several moments. I will never forget the strength I received from her. Wanting to believe her, I tried to pull myself together.

At that moment, our friend Sherri wandered down the hall for a visit. The smile on her face evaporated as she found me. One of the nurses must have brought her up to speed. She pulled me to her and led me back to the same waiting room where I had waited a half hour earlier. This time there was no talk of discharge.

"Is he going to die?" I asked her as she pressed me into the nearest sofa and sat beside me. We could have passed for sisters with our dark hair, dark eyes and small 5'2" frames. Sherri had just completed her nursing degree at age 50. Eye level with me, she began to explain.

"No, Judy, he's not going to die. They are re-intubating him. His lungs must be too weak to breathe on their own. He is going to pull through. They'll let us know when you can go back and see him."

"The social worker was just here talking about discharge. I don't understand. What happened? I don't know how much more he can take! You should have seen his eyes! Sherri, he was terrified!"

She hugged me tightly and waited through my next round of sobs. "Sometimes it takes a few tries. It's going to get better."

"They can do it again?"

"Oh yes. They will probably try again in a few days once he's stronger."

Our synagogue rabbi appeared as Sherri returned me to an outward semblance of calm. They waited with me, their presence giving me strength. A short time later Betsy came to get me.

"He's doing fine. You can come see him now," she said.

Sherri and I hurried down the hall. I felt a profound sense of relief, but it was held in check by the sad look on Mel's face. My heart broke for him; he didn't get a chance to speak that day. Mel's lungs were not able to inflate sufficiently, and the doctors were concerned. With his level of spinal cord injury, it was expected that Mel would be able to breathe independently, but nothing was for certain. Everything below the point of injury was up for grabs. We tried to remain hopeful for the future.

Sherri left after a few minutes, noting our need to be alone. The sounds of the ventilator filled the space; Mel and I looked at each other, both saddened by the reminder. With breathing independently put on temporary hold, we focused our efforts elsewhere that day.

"You know what Mel? I think I'll read some of the CaringBridge comments. What do you think?"

He opened his eyes wide and nodded.

***

The day had been endless, and I was still reeling from the extubation fiasco. Pam sat me down and watched me eat in a conference room on the other side of the hospital, where amazingly, the Jewish hospital staff had a well-stocked refrigerator with kosher food available to anyone who needed it. Once I had eaten enough to satisfy my BFF, she marched me back to Mel to say goodnight. Holding my arm for physical as well as emotional support, Pam and I walked the half-block to the parking garage.

"I'll follow you home," she said.

"No, don't worry, I'll be fine," I assured her when we got to my car. She hugged me and waited for me to get in. I lowered my window and heard her call, "Get some sleep," as she turned the corner headed toward her car.

I'll try, I thought, as I buckled my seatbelt.

I paid for the day's parking and headed out of the garage. I turned left and made my way to the first right. I couldn't decide which way to turn. Choosing right, I started down the street, still unclear if I was going in the right direction. But I immediately saw my mistake because cars were headed

45

directly toward me! I quickly pulled into a side alley breathing deeply. Oh My God! Was that a one-way street? I panicked. Pulling out my smartphone I tapped and tapped, trying to find the GPS. A full minute later I found it and shaking, typed in our home address.

I waited for the GPS voice to direct me and started to pull out carefully. I listened to the GPS and made a few turns, but nothing looked right. I couldn't keep up with the GPS commands and began to realize I was missing the turns. I knew it shouldn't be so difficult to make my way to route 83, the downtown expressway. Confusion and exhaustion are a combustible combination. I found myself going the wrong way on one-way streets three times in the space of ten minutes. Starting to sweat and close to tears, I pulled into a parking space and listened to my rapid heartbeat. How am I ever going to make it home? Trying to focus, I tapped at the phone some more until I found the step-by-step directions. I read them slowly over and over.

I can do this.

I must do this.

It's only a few turns.

I pulled out of the parking space hesitantly and began to drive once again. I used my last few ounces of reserve concentration power and somehow managed to follow the directions.

Breathing a huge sigh of relief, I finally found the expressway. I knew it was only a 15-minute drive from that point, a drive I had done many, many times while working in the city. Not trusting myself, I stayed in the right lane and drove at minimum speed. Thankfully I managed the rest of the drive without incident. Rounding the corner into our cul-de-sac, I breathed another huge sigh of relief. I made it! I knew it was a miracle. I headed into the house and closed the door behind me. Sinking to the floor, I began to sob. What had I done? How stupid can one person be? What would Mel do if I got myself killed?

I sat there for a while until I was able to pull myself together and walked up to our bedroom. I changed and sat down heavily on the bed thinking: It was clear to me that I was incapable of driving myself. Whom could I call at this hour? Who would be available to drive me first thing the next morning? The answer came to me in a flash: Phran, our neighbor and close friend. I knew I could count on her, and sure enough she came through. I relied on friends and family to drive me to the hospital morning and evening for the next full week.

Reinventing the Wheel

Mel certainly was not the first patient at Shock Trauma, and he certainly was not the first person to suffer a spinal cord injury. But sometimes we felt that we were reinventing the wheel, needing to use creativity and ingenuity to handle daily issues and challenges.

Mel couldn't speak. He was intubated. Anyone who has ever been intubated or has seen someone intubated knows that there is no way for an intubated person to speak. So other means of communication are essential.

By the middle of the first week after the accident, Mel was anxious to communicate. He needed to ask his own questions, get his own answers and express his worries and his thoughts. Using one of the few movements in his small repertoire, we found that he could blink as I recited the alphabet. I watched his eyes, and he would blink as I reached the correct letter. Although a painfully slow process, it did work. Mel showed incredible focus and perseverance, as letter by letter he would spell his words, then his sentences and sometimes his jokes. This was no easy task in his condition but guessing his next letter or word became a game of sorts for those surrounding his bed. Mel and I don't share the same sense of humor, so jokes that were very funny to his visitors were somewhat frustrating for me, often taking a long time to spell. Still it was amazing that he maintained his sense of humor, and I was grateful for that.

I did have one small – well, not really so small problem. I found myself getting sick by the end of that first week with a severe sore throat, a precursor to a full-blown cold. This made each repetition of the alphabet painful. As I looked around at our small group of visitors who were enthralled with the success of our little routine, I wondered if anyone else would try it. I knew it was my job to be Mel's advocate and voice, so I symbolically gave him mine at this time. By the end of the day on Friday my vocal chords were battered. Lots of hot tea for me over the weekend.

The next time Mel's inpatient OT appeared early in the second week, she noticed our communication technique. Suggesting a written chart, she found clean paper and a marker. She rigged up a pointer that fit into Mel's left wrist brace since he was able to move his left arm up and down. This method proved exhausting. His arm tired after a few movements, and the angle of the paper was difficult for him to see and reach.

I kept thinking that we were certainly not the first and would certainly not be the last to have this communication issue. Why keep reinventing the wheel? Why wasn't there an assortment of tools and techniques available to help us? There may have been, but it was only through persistence that Mel was given some. By prodding the OT, we were able to get her to dig into her bag of tricks. She brought Mel a big red button that he could easily press, much like the Easy Button in the Staples commercial, and attached it to the left side of Mel's hospital gown within range of his left forearm. A small arm movement could produce the intended effect, a call to the nurse. This occurred deep into the second week post-accident.

Time Out

Freeze-frame, I wanted to shout. We need a few minutes here.

It had been almost a full week of the craziness, the frantic, frenzied pace, much like living life in perpetual fast-forward mode. Nurses moved in and out of the room, monitoring Mel's progress, adjusting Mel's various tubes, drips and cushions, administering a multitude of medicines, including the neuroprotective steroids which kept Mel's spinal cord from further traumatic disruption. Doctors moved in and out, checking, assessing, and planning, performing the procedures that were needed. Although I had gotten the word out and had severely limited visitation, our core group of friends and family joined us often. The comings and goings of all were well-meaning, life-affirming, medically necessary, but unfortunately, unrelenting.

On Thursday morning, I sent a group text out. "Please allow us a few hours, from 11-1, to rest. We need some quiet time. We love you all. Just need a few minutes." To be honest, I was coming unglued. Sore throat aside, I probably looked almost as haggard as Mel. Not a pretty sight.

Our friend Neil was the one person most upset by this request. Extremely busy and successful in his psychology practice, his primary office was near the hospital, and his lunch hour was his only break until late at night. "Please, just allow Neil to come," Pam pleaded, texting me right away.

"Tomorrow. Not today. Please tell him I'm so sorry," I wrote back. Asserting myself was not an easy thing to do, but

I was done in. Mel – well, I was sure quiet time would work for him as well.

Mel's nurse transferred him from bed to chair while I went down the hall and got some tea. He was propped up on a big seat cushion in an upright sturdy chair when I returned. The two hours, the allotted and required time for him to work on sitting, had begun. Placing my hot cup on the food service table beside him, I lugged a similar chair around the room, positioning it opposite Mel. Plopping down, I faced him with a small smile. "Alone at last," I said quietly reaching for my tea, inhaling the sweet herbal scent. Taking a sip, I closed my eyes and listened. Hums and beeps from the machines, the sound of the ventilator, distant footsteps in the hallway. Putting the tea back on the table, I settled into the chair, bringing my knees to my chest. Mel's eyes were closed, and he appeared relatively comfortable. I took the moment for what it was, a gift.

Shabbat #2

It was almost time for our second Shabbat. Late that Friday afternoon, Gary brought me to the hotel just a few short blocks from the hospital. Dropping my hastily packed bag by the door I walked in with relief, ever grateful to Gary for making all the arrangements for me. I faced a few brief moments of quiet, a short respite from the confines of the hospital, and a space of time to notice how sick I felt both physically and emotionally. With a heavy plop, I sank into the armchair by the bed and took a number of deep belly breaths, summoning up my yoga training to help relax.

It was then I noticed a big package in the center of the bed. I reached over and pulled the cellophane-wrapped montage closer. Tears filled my eyes as I realized that the care package containing assorted toiletries, snacks, books, magazines and other goodies was from Jewish Caring Network, a Baltimore based nonprofit organization dedicated to providing support services to families facing life-threatening, lifelong or serious illnesses.[1]

I guess that's us, I thought. We now fit the criteria, I realized with a jolt. Putting that acknowledgement safely in the back of my mind, where it needed to be for me to move forward, I got up and headed to the shower. To say that my throat ached would be an understatement. Lack of sleep, worry, and overall exhaustion had turned what could have been a springtime cold into another big worry. I could barely speak without wincing, yet speak I did all day long for myself

---

[1] http://jewishcaringnetwork.org

as well as for Mel. I was Mel's mouthpiece as he tried valiantly to communicate with the staff and visitors. We had found a way to communicate using a very limited list of things at our disposal: my voice, Mel's blink, and a lot of patience. Even though we had severely limited visitation and asked for the understanding of all Mel's well-wishers – which probably numbered in the hundreds – the day was filled with constant activity, and his need to be heard and understood was paramount.

So, as I showered and the water sluiced down my body bringing momentary relief to my exhausted outer wrapping, inside I trembled with worry. How was I going to hold on myself? I thought, wretchedly. Turning so that my throat was positioned in the fullest stream of water, I let myself wallow.

After a few minutes of self-pity I started to instruct myself.

You can do it, you must do it.

You can do it, you must do it, I repeated as a mantra for the next few minutes, until I was steady enough to convince myself to try and believe it.

Enough. Clamping down on my own trivial needs I turned my thoughts to Mel, and that's all the incentive I needed. Purposefully, I stepped out of the shower much sooner than I wanted because I needed to hurry to get back to Mel in time to start Shabbat. This week he would be lucid. Gary would join us alone because his wife, Sherri, was out of town for the weekend, and the three of us would manage to bring a semblance of Shabbat to the miserable situation. I got dressed quickly and moved the JCN package to the chair, silently thanking them for the kindness. I would make good use of the package contents over the next few weeks.

I started the second Shabbat as I did the first. I turned off Mel's hospital room lights by flicking the switch to the down position. Then, I announced to Gary and Mel that I was starting Shabbat as I moved the switch to the up position. No candles, no blessing, just two beautiful men watching and joining me.

Clad in nice navy slacks, a white button-down shirt and knitted yarmulke, Gary alternately stood and sat by Mel's bedside as he prayed with him. Gary is an emotional guy. As I watched them from the back of the room where I was resting, I noticed Gary's deep set brown eyes fill with tears. Catching my attention, and not the least bit embarrassed by the show of emotion, Gary pointed to Mel. "He is mouthing the words." As I got up to look, I did indeed see Mel mouthing the words, his eyes closed in concentration. I don't think either one of us will ever forget that sight.

Later, Gary and I set a makeshift Shabbat table at Mel's bedside, filled with the plentiful, tasty food sent again by *Bikur Cholim*. We ate a quick dinner while Mel rested. We felt sad that Mel could not eat with us, but he communicated by shaking his head that he wanted us nearby and was comforted by our presence. Even so, we didn't linger over the meal; it seemed rather cruel. We cleaned up and watched as the nurse prepared Mel for the night. I discussed Mel's routine and needs with the night nurse and helped him get settled before heading back to the hotel.

As I fell into bed, I mentally reviewed the highs and lows of the week.

The highs: Mel's surgeries were successful and he didn't seem to be having any post-surgery issues; he successfully passed the critical one-week mark in which the spinal cord was susceptible to further injury. Neuroprotective drugs had been used to reduce the possibility of additional trauma, a background worry that I don't think Mel or I shared with anyone, yet this was a huge relief. He seemed to have some good movement in his left arm and some small movement in his left leg, which did bode well. His spirits remained high, and he was able to crack jokes and make me smile, which I found incredible.

The lows: the failed extubation left everyone worried, and there was no date scheduled for another try. The constant need for suctioning and respiratory treatments kept Mel from getting any real rest; communication was beyond difficult and he and I were both getting frustrated; plus, his muscles had atrophied to nothing and we still had no idea if his entire right side was paralyzed.

Tomorrow is another day, I thought. As I let exhaustion take over, I was thankful for the good friends who were watching out for us and anticipating our needs with such love. Silently thanking Gary again, I sunk into the comfort of the plush bed. My brain and body had had enough. I slept. I prayed that Mel was doing the same.

Tracheostomy Decision

Days 8-9

May 12, 2013

Mel wishes Yom Ha'aim Samayach to all! Mel is still waiting to resolve the breathing issue and his patience and fortitude are truly incredible. Shabbat was another day of healing and he was able to find some rest. We thank Gary B. for sharing Shabbat with us and for sharing the miracles as Mel mouthed L'cha Dodi and davened with much kavana. The big improvement today is increased mobility in the right leg. This is big! I would like to thank Bikur Cholim and Jewish Caring Network for providing for my needs throughout the week and for Shabbat. Amazing kindness I will never forget!

It was a busy and eventful weekend for Mel, and we were grateful to have Devon as his nurse for both days. From the first moment when he walked in with assurance and purpose, I knew he would be good for Mel. Devon reminded me so much of a young cousin in the family who is also a male nurse, with his solid medium build, dark hair and eyes, strength of character and no-nonsense approach to his profession. Intuitively, I knew I could trust him to help me with the most difficult decision I had had to date; whether to go forward with a tracheostomy or to wait.

The intubation countdown had begun; it was becoming increasingly more dangerous to continue to be intubated, the risks too great for infection and weakness. The medical staff had recommended and scheduled the tracheostomy, a procedure to place a tube into Mel's trachea to help him breathe and allow him to come off the ventilator. But the exact time of the tracheostomy was not determined; the schedule was tight and the doctor was booked throughout the day. She was hoping to fit Mel in at the end of her weekend shift.

Jack and Ron, those to whom I turned for my medical understanding and guidance, didn't agree on this issue. "It's another surgery, not a thing to be taken lightly," Dr. Ron had warned me. "Give it a few more days." Jack understood it differently and told me that it was normal protocol. In addition, the medical staff assigned to Mel's case all thought it was the way to go. Mel was miserable with the intubation and in dire need of a change, but it remained unclear whether he could be successfully extubated. He was getting stronger and we saw movement on his right side that very day – a huge development that opened up all new possibilities!

As the day progressed with our core group coming and going, the back area of Mel's room was in constant flux. We discussed the surgery throughout. Early in the afternoon, our middle daughter Shana, son-in-law Moshe and grandson Akiva arrived from Israel to be with us. "We're coming," Shana had told me earlier that week, allowing no argument. Our middle daughter went to Israel after high school. Living the dream, she earned a college degree, met her wonderful husband Moshe and built a beautiful life in Israel. The only problem is the 6000 miles and seven-hour time difference that makes her feel so far away. Skype and phone calls are our lifeline. Without hesitation, Shana and Moshe left their jobs, school and responsibilities to be with us for two and half weeks. Their need to be with us was as strong as our need to be with them. Immediately, their presence brought us new hope and light. Hugging Shana tightly, I conveyed our gratitude and relief that she and her family were home with us. That day I was even able to carve out a few amazing minutes running after two-year old Akiva in the mini urban park outside the hospital. What a joy amidst it all!

The decision was still there when I returned to Mel's room. It hung over my head the entire day, and I turned to our day nurse again and again asking him to describe the details of the tracheostomy and why the staff seemed settled on the matter. The A team, the surgical team, came to speak to us briefly. We had agreed to proceed with the tracheostomy, but only because we did not know that extubation was still a possibility. As the day progressed so did my sense of worry. I imagined the doctor performing surgery after surgery all weekend, her exhaustion growing as she worked through her second consecutive day. Mel needed to breathe more easily. He needed to be disconnected from the miserable ventilator. He needed to communicate. He needed all of it NOW!

Nurse Devon listened to my concerns, surely noting my growing agitation. I asked him what he would do for his loved one. Though he knew that the tracheostomy was the regular protocol in this type of case and would make it easier for the nursing staff, he finally gave me the words I needed.

"You don't need to make a decision today," Devon said. "You can hold off until tomorrow and speak to the medical team again. You can ask them if extubation is possible."

And that is what I did. I know that the medical staff was very confused that I had postponed the surgery, but I did get our meeting first thing the next day. Actually Mel's situation was not clear-cut. The A Team senior doctor sat down with Mel and me. She told us that she honestly did not know how Mel would do if we tried another extubation. She thought he might do well, but she just was not sure. Conversely, she assured us that Mel would definitely succeed with the tracheostomy; it was a safer and more predictable route. Although somewhat disappointed, Mel and I were satisfied that all the options had been discussed more thoroughly. In addition, the lead doctor guaranteed us that she would do the surgery herself at the first opportunity. Unfortunately, the first free operating room time she could schedule wasn't until the next day. Mel's extended suffering, 36 hours of additional time on the ventilator, weighed heavily on me; I was almost as miserable as he was through the long and difficult hours.

May 13, 2013

Take a moment and just breathe. That is the hurdle we are facing. Mel's breathing is going well, but he needs a small assist from the ventilator. The time when the safety of intubation from infection has passed, therefore Mel will need an operation today to insert a small tube into his trachea, a temporary tracheostomy. This will allow Mel to finally talk and eat while providing breathing support as needed. This is progress, and Mel is looking forward to the advantages. Please continue to daven and learn on his behalf especially today as he faces another operation.

***

First thing Tuesday morning the head doctor performed the surgery. The seemingly simple surgery was successful but there were complications. I think that Dr. Ron realized the inherent risks. I did heed his advice by holding off, although I didn't force another extubation attempt. Without assurances, we just couldn't chance another failure. With the surgery issue settled and done, Mel progressed quickly. All in all, it was a good choice.

I send my everlasting gratitude to our patient and kind Devon.

May 14, 2013

Breathing — what can I say? It is such a bracha. In a shiur I attended this past winter, Rabbi Silber explained that when we exhale the nishama (soul) tries to escape our bodies and return to Hashem, but Hashem tells the nishama that it is not time and sends the nishama back with the next inhale. As I watch Mel on his first trial with the trach collar passing the half hour mark without support from the vent and breathing comfortably totally on his own, I know that Hashem has plans for my dear husband. His nishama has much to do. May Hashem continue to bless him with forward progress. Today is a good day, and I am breathing better myself. A few people have told me that Hashem healed everyone with Matan Torah. May this continue to be so and may all who are ill or injured be healed this Shavuot. Please keep Mel close to your hearts as you learn this Chag and Chag samayach to all!

Mel Is Not There

Shana and I walked briskly the few short blocks to the hospital. Nearly on time, I thought as we entered the hallway to Mel's room at 8:40 a.m. I could still hear little Shira pleading, "Stay with me Savta; I don't want you to go." Becca, Simcha, their girls and Shana had stayed over with me in a nearby hotel. For the Jewish holiday of Shavuot, the holiday in which we celebrate the giving of the Torah, we have many of the same observances of Shabbat, and we had gathered close. Shira, a sad little frown on her face, held my hand and refused to let go. "I want you to play with me," she said. Thinking that the one thing that could top her wanting to play with me was how much I wanted to play with her, I looked into the disappointed, precious brown eyes of our four-year old granddaughter.

With a leaden heart, I squatted down to her level. "Shira, my love, Saba needs me in the hospital. I will try to come back later for a little while and play with you. He is all alone, but you have Mommy, Daddy and Eliora with you." With a big hug and kiss, I gently pulled myself away. "I'll see you later. Maybe we can play a bit then," I said, hoping somehow it may be possible. Becca came to console her as I turned away.

Shana patted my back as we entered the stairwell. "She'll be fine. Don't worry," she told me as we trudged along the short blocks to the hospital.

Resolutely, I entered Mel's room, Shana just a step behind. "Mel, how are you?" I asked brightly as I approached his bed. "How was your night?"

A cold chill filled me as I looked him over. Vacant blue, glassy eyes met mine. Instinctively, I was on high alert. Where was my Mel? His body was there, but the "real" Mel was missing. My heart thumped when he didn't answer my inquiries. I nearly flew out of the room looking for a nurse.

"What's wrong, Mom?" Shana asked.

"He's not there!" I answered panicked.

Confused, Shana watched me run out the door.

My agitation duly noted, I was quickly directed to Mel's nurse of the day. In short order, she explained that Mel had a rampant urinary infection for which he was already being treated. I had heard that confusion and altered states are known symptoms of UTIs, especially in the elderly. But Mel was not elderly, nor had he been sick until this infection. I worried that a whole new slew of problems were on the horizon.

We stayed by Mel's side throughout the day; Shana, Becca and I made sure someone was nearby. Lost and uncertain, it was one of the most trying days for me during the whole long recovery. I felt Mel's absence and missed him. Except for the surgeries when he was unconscious, Mel had been mentally sound throughout. My partner in life was with me, even if his body was broken. For the first time since the crisis began, I felt separated from him; I felt he had left me, and I was unsure if he would return.

Noting my distress and growing fatigue, the girls convinced me to take a break in the afternoon. I backtracked to the hotel a few blocks from the hospital to try to rest. The challenges of the week made my steps heavy. As I settled into bed, I heard a little knock on my door. Having just returned from a walk in the city with her father and sister, Shira peeked her head in. "Savta, you're back," she said.

"Yes. For a little while. Come on in," I told her. "Do you want to cuddle with me?"

Not having to be asked twice, she quickly crossed the short distance to the bed and climbed in.

"Tell me a story," she said.

"Not today, precious. I am so tired. Can we rest a bit?"

My intuitive little buddy settled herself under my arm and said, "You rest, Savta. I'll tell you a story."

Smiling, I listened to her, the words flowing over me little a warm shower.

Simcha called to Shira, worried that she was bothering me. Just the opposite, I assured him. Shira had given me the perfect rest; she had lightened my heart. My respite was over. It was time to return to the hospital.

I found Mel still unfocused and altered when I returned. Shira had given me hope, but the sight of Mel brought me to tears. The girls comforted me and gave me the strength and support to get me through the rest of that horrible day, never leaving my side.

***

The next morning I rushed into Mel's room. Palms sweaty, I slowly looked him over, finally meeting his eyes hesitantly. Relief flooded through me. Bright, focused, gorgeous blue eyes gave me the answer I needed. The antibiotics had started to clear the infection. Mel was back! Our first medical complication was almost behind us. Unfortunately, it would not be our last.

Day 14

May 17, 2013

Mel faced new challenges throughout Yom Tov but with herculean strength and incredible resolve, he made some real progress. Today, after he patiently listened to the surgeon's assessment, he mouthed, "If Rachel M. could do this sick, I can do this healthy." Rachel, a beautiful young woman who taught so many of us how to live with unbelievable grace and determination as she struggled for years with cancer, continues to inspire. Mel is gaining chizuk from her life and memory. Mel is injured but healthy. The road is long but doable. May he continue to find strength for all the horrific and inhuman demands that he faces daily. Please continue to daven for him. We truly appreciate all the learning over Yom Tov on his behalf. Shabbat Shalom.

Acinetobacter

With the urinary infection under control, we moved on to the third Shabbat post-accident. Medical school and nursing school graduations made logistics difficult. Hotel rooms near the hospital were scarce, but I persevered. Using the hospital discount I booked what seemed to be the last two rooms available. We ended the week on a high note; Mel was back, alert and clear-minded. Although Becca and family had returned to New Jersey, Shana, Moshe and Akiva were joining me for Shabbat.

Once again, *Bikur Cholim* provided an abundance of tasty food, which Shana, Moshe and I enjoyed in a makeshift alcove configured by opening up the closet door and outside door, bringing them together to a point, and thereby sectioning off the room to allow little two-year old Akiva to sleep undisturbed. With our mood positive, the area cozy, we enjoyed a brief break from the continual drama.

***

I gathered myself early and headed to the door. I looked back longingly at the upscale hotel room and comfy bed. I had passed a remarkably restful night, a novelty these days, and wished for just a moment that I could crawl back in. Shaking my head, I closed the door behind me. I stopped by Shana, Moshe and Akiva's room down the hall to tell them that I was heading to the hospital. After agreeing that Shana would follow shortly, I walked quickly out of the hotel, down the two blocks and across another three and arrived at the hospital by my daily 8:30 a.m. deadline.

Circumventing the system, I flashed my paper neon pink visitor bracelet still intact from the day before at the guard and made a quick left turn followed by a sharp right. I walked down the long corridor, moving close to the wall as a gurney was pushed past me. The hospital staff attempted to quiet an irate patient alternately moaning and yelling to be released. I empathized with the patient, barely restraining my own wish to be free of the hospital and the need to be there. I rushed to the far end of the building and up the four flights of stairs. Careening to a stop, I took a deep breath and waited for the electronic double doors to swing wide and admit me. It was Shabbat and I couldn't press the bell on the wall for admittance. I anxiously waited for someone to come along and either press the bell or swipe a hospital pass. After a few long minutes the door magically opened. I neared my goal, Mel in room number 8, at the end of the hall. I pulled the curtain to his room and started to enter.

"You cannot go in there without gown and gloves," a nurse unknown to me announced.

"What?" I asked confused.

"Gown and gloves. Here – I will get you some," she continued, moving to a storage shelf across the hall.

Confused but compliant, I asked, "Why do I need a gown all of a sudden?"

"Your nurse will be in to explain in a minute," she replied.

"Can I go in now?"

"Yes. I'll tell your nurse that you're here."

I entered Mel's room. What now? I thought. I quickly assessed the situation, my eyes automatically scanning the display and then resting on Mel – oxygen saturation levels good, Mel alert and sitting up.

"How are you? How was your night?" I asked him moving close to the bed and touching his hand. He responded by nodding his head.

I walked over to the counter to look for the alphabet page, our current form of communication, but stopped as a nurse entered the room.

"Your husband's lab results have come back and have been found positive for *Acinetobacter*, an infectious disease that is highly resistant to many antibiotics. For your safety, you need to gown and glove upon entering the room. Come with me and I'll go over the procedures with you. When you leave the room, you'll need to remove the gown and gloves and use hand sanitizer on your hands."

I looked to Mel, but I could not intuit his thoughts from such a distance. Always the good soldier, I followed as instructed.

The nurse filled a cubicle just outside of Mel's room with supplies, explained the procedures again and helped me prepare for re-entry to the room.

"Is Mel sick with this disease?" I asked.

"He has been exposed to it and the doctors have him on antibiotics for the urinary tract infection, so he should be fine."

"How did this happen? Is he going to get better?"

"We do our best not to spread this infection, but it is common in the hospital setting. He is on the appropriate antibiotics for the urinary infection and for the *Acinetobacter*. We are doing what should be done."

Mind spinning, I rubbed my temples to ward off the sudden headache forming between my eyes. I began to panic, "Is it contagious? My daughter is expecting, and she will be in to visit soon. Is it all right for her to be here?"

"She should be fine. It's dangerous for people with weakened immune systems."

"Are you sure? I don't want her exposed if there is risk to her or the baby. I need to know for sure."

"I'll get the head nurse to come in and speak to you, to reassure you."

"I would appreciate that."

Dr. A., the head of the medical team arrived minutes later and reiterated that Mel had been exposed due to his compromised state and that he was being treated. All visitors and staff were required to take the precautions of gowning and gloving, the normal protocol. We would not experience any ill effects – our immune systems were healthy. The mother and baby would be fine. The doctor did not feel there was any reason to keep Shana from visiting. She also said that exposure the day before when both my pregnant daughters had been visiting was no cause for concern.

How to explain the pit in my stomach, the despondency that threatened to sink me? Just the day before, I had breathed relief that Mel was responding to the antibiotics for the severe urinary infection. Medical complications piled on top of the uncertainty of Mel's recovery; I tried to grapple with this new development. I looked over at Mel; his face remained passive. I was on my own with this one.

To say I was worried is certainly an understatement. Had it been any day but Shabbat, I would have jumped on the phone calling for clarification from all the doctors I knew or could find to discuss the topic, simultaneously scouring the Internet for details until I was completely satisfied that I was sufficiently informed. But it was Shabbat, and as an Orthodox Jew, I did not use electronic devices on the day of rest. I could not call Dr. Ron or Jack for advice or look up this dreaded disease on a computer. I made another difficult choice; I chose to believe the doctors and nurses. When Shana arrived, I informed her, helped her to gown and glove up and prayed that all would be well, she and the baby unharmed. My prayers were constant as was my need to adjust my thinking, make decisions no one should be forced to make and handle an endless stream of challenges.

I would love to conclude my account of the day here, but eventually the sun set on the third Shabbat. As Shana and I were about to leave for the evening, the night nurse appeared. He was horrified to find Shana and me in Mel's room.

"Have you been here all day?" he asked.

"Yes. We stayed gowned and gloved," I responded quickly.

"Didn't they tell you that your husband has been infected with *Acinetobacter*?"

"Yes. Dr. A. told me it was okay. She said there was no serious risk."

"Well, I would never let my daughter or wife come into this infected room!" he exclaimed abruptly staring us down.

I glanced over and saw Shana's dismayed expression, certainly reflective of my own. Not knowing what else to do, we continued gathering our things. I worried about Mel's emotional state as we said goodbye for the evening. What was he thinking? How terrible it must have been for him to hear the sickening outburst and know that he did nothing to cause this terrible situation, nor that he could do anything to change it or protect any of us from the consequences. The old adage, "Hospitals make you sick" came to mind. Mel was healthy and strong before the accident. He was injured, not sick. The sudden medical complications were hospital-based, not injury-based.

Anxiously, I got Shana out of there as quickly as possible. As she related the new worries to Moshe, I felt despair that threatened to break me. Bless him, our wise son-in-law listened carefully, maintained his outward composure and kept any negative thoughts to himself. If either he or Shana had lost their cool, I don't know how I would have hung in myself.

Once home, I called Jack for support. As always, he quelled my worries with assurances that *Acinetobacter*, although a terrible disease that fails to respond to many antibiotics, was a constant in the hospital setting. All health care professionals face it every day and many are carriers with no serious ramifications. He agreed with Dr. A.; Shana and I were healthy, her fetus was safe within her healthy body and all would be well. He was direct and confident and that worked for me. Without Jack, I surely would not have slept a wink that night or many to follow. After relaying Jack's sentiments to Shana and Moshe, I gave up for the day, hoping that the challenges of the next would be somehow kinder.

***

The *Acinetobacter* issue remained with us for weeks. I feared that Mel would not get adequate care and opportunities during his therapy sessions at Kernan, the rehabilitation hospital we chose. I worried that he would not be allowed to participate fully. The scary-looking infectious sign on his doorway at Shock Trauma and later Kernan raised a red flag for all who entered. The gowning and gloving routine was a constant annoyance during the dreadful summer heat of Baltimore. However, Mel's therapy and treatment were not outwardly affected.

Mysteriously, about three weeks later, the sign came down, the gloves and gowns came off, and no one mentioned *Acinetobacter* again.

Tracheostomy Collar Trial

With the urinary infection under control and the *Acinetobacter* a background reality, the focus returned to recovery from the injury. Mel had a new challenge. He needed to breathe effectively through the tracheostomy tube. Oxygen was directed into the tube, and the tube was held in place with a trach collar. For 48 hours, he was carefully monitored to make sure his oxygen saturation level did not dip below the low 90s. I sat by his side much of the weekend, head upturned, staring at the monitor above his bed. Thankfully there were no complications, and 48 hours grew to 50 and beyond. The trach collar trial was a success, and Mel was ready for release to Kernan Rehabilitation Institute.[2]

Kernan, one of the nation's leading rehabilitation hospitals for spinal cord injuries, was one of two hospitals in the area that could handle tracheostomy patients. (Although I had an opportunity to look further.) Our cousin Malka had spoken to her brother in New Jersey, and he had connected me with the medical director at Kessler Institute for Rehabilitation, the number two hospital for spinal cord injury located in New Jersey.

Dr. K. was extremely receptive to my call. We discussed options and he urged us to remain in Baltimore. "I know some of the staff at Kernan," he said. "Your husband will get great care. Stay where you have support from family, friends and community." I heeded his advice. His heartfelt "Please

---

[2] Changed during Mel's stay to the University of Maryland Rehabilitation and Orthopoedic Institute -Ed.

know that you can always bring your husband here. Just call me if you have any problems," warmed my heart and gave us confidence. In fact, I did call him weeks later with a few questions. His receptivity and caring made a profound impact on us.

Day 16

May 19, 2013

Shabbat was another day of healing. Although certainly not a regular Shabbat in any way, Mel got a chance to rest more than usual without some of the constant activity. With utmost gratitude to Hashem, each day he continues to improve, and he has reached the 25-hour mark in trach collar trials. A big milestone and a big step toward moving to rehab will be reaching 48 hours. Please daven for Mel to hit this milestone with strength.

Dysphagia

As one challenge was resolved, another immediately took the forefront. Swallowing was Mel's next hurdle. Swallowing dysfunction, or dysphagia, is a common complication following a cervical spinal cord injury. The ability to swallow is necessary for two vital functions: to help with eating and drinking and to prevent aspiration. Aspiration is when material such as food, fluid or the contents of the stomach enters the respiratory tract. The act of normal swallowing involves the extraordinary coordination and sequencing of more than 25 pairs of muscles in the mouth, pharynx, larynx and esophagus.[3] All the neural pathways in Mel's body had been jolted by the injury to his spinal cord. His muscles had no strength or muscle memory. He had dysphagia.

A speech therapist was assigned to Mel's team to determine the extent of the problem and to begin therapy. She performed a barium swallow test. The results were definitive. His muscles were too weak and he was only allowed to have small ice chips, three per hour, in a meager attempt to quench his rampant thirst. It had been 16 days since Mel had anything to drink. His thirst preoccupied him. His thirst preoccupied me. He begged for ice chips, and the hours dragged on while he waited with patience I would surely not have had. The look on his face as he savored each

---

[3] Cunningham ET., Jr, Donner MW., Jones B., Point SM. Anatomical and physiological overview In: Jones B., Donner MW., eds. Normal and Abnormal Swallowing. Imaging in Diagnosis and Therapy. Berlin: Springer-Verlag; 1991:7– 32 http://www.ncbi.nlm.nih.gov/pmc/articles/PMC3584789

chip can only be described as rapturous. Then it was gone, and the wait for the next morsel was excruciating. Mel dreamed of devouring his two favorites – Slurpees and Rita's ices.

Day 17

May 20, 2013

Today we are delighted that Mel has surpassed the 53-hour mark for the trach collar trial!!! Breathing gets a big check mark as we move on to the next of infinite challenges.

Waiting is difficult at the best of times. Waiting to eat or drink after a fast of 25 hours is often challenging. But the waiting that Mel is doing in order to drink after 16 days is incomprehensible. In a little over an hour Mel will have a test to determine if his swallowing capability at this point in time will allow fluids to travel down his esophagus instead of the dangerous path to his lungs through his trachea. His injury and surgeries make this a hurdle that must be jumped. All he desires is a Slurpee and honestly that is the only thing he has asked for since this all began. He says a Rita's ice would be okay too. May Hashem grant him this simple request today. I can't wait to make the mad dash to 7-eleven!

Mel Speaks

With the high of the trach collar trial and the low of the failed swallowing test still fresh in our minds, we began a new day. Mid-morning, Mel's speech therapist returned with exciting news. We discussed Mel's ability to speak. She explained that Mel's tracheostomy would soon be fitted with a speaking valve attached to the tip of the tracheostomy tube. This one-way valve allows air to pass into the tracheostomy but not through it and opens as the patient breathes in. The air that is inhaled goes around the tracheostomy tube and up through the vocal chords which allows the patient to make sounds. The wearer then breathes out through the mouth and nose rather than through the tracheostomy. The sounds that are created give the patient an altered but understandable voice.[4]

The therapist returned with the valve within hours, trying a few for size. With Yael by my side, we watched and listened as Mel took a deep breath and then uttered his first sounds, his first words in over two weeks. We listened as his precious voice flowed out to us after being silenced for 18 days. The tears filled our eyes as his vocal chords fired and the valve did its job.

"I love you."

Three simple words, the most perfect sound to our ears.

Day18

---

[4]http:/www.hopkinsmedicine.org/tracheostomy/living/passey-muir_valve.html

May 21, 2013

Today is a record day! Although Mel has to wait a little longer for his Slurpees, he continues to breathe with ease. This morning he displayed fine motor skill by moving some of the fingers on both hands – an incredible achievement at this early stage. Then he spoke for the first time in 18 days through a fitted speaking valve on his trach. I got teary when I heard his sweet voice for the first time in so long. Then the speech therapist became teary watching me. The biggest news is that as I write this we are waiting for transport to transfer Mel to rehab at Kernan Hospital! This should happen in the next hour. His progress is amazing and today he was more awake and alert than ever before. We believe that your prayers are spurring him on. Knowing so many people care and are thinking about him and us is extremely comforting. The staff here all believe Mel is a Rock Star and we all know that it is true.

Not in Kansas Anymore

Shana and I walked across a long parking lot whose whole front section is marked handicapped, and through a set of sliding double doors into Kernan Rehabilitation Hospital. I rolled my army-green overnight bag to the front counter. We were directed right past the reception desk, straight down a long corridor, then left to the Spinal Cord Injury unit. We took in the wide, clean and quiet hallways at 7:30 in the evening. I positioned myself in front of the receptionist.

"Where is Mel Pachino's room?"

"He isn't here yet, but you can wait in his room," she replied.

"Not here?" I asked. Do you know when he will be here? We left him hours ago and were told transport was on its way."

"He should be here any time now," she said. "I'll show you to his room. You can wait there."

"Thanks," I said disappointedly, as Shana and I rushed to follow her down the hall and around a turn to a corner room at the end of the corridor. She left us quickly to return to her station.

Shana and I looked at each other.

"Here we are," I said.

"He'll be here soon, Mom," she said in an effort to comfort me.

"I hope so."

I rolled my bag past a storage closet and counter with a sink to a space between two chairs that were set up beneath two wide corner windows. We sat down facing the empty bed wearing identical worried expressions on our faces. I noted the built in shelving units on each side of the bed, end tables of sorts.

Where is Mel? I wondered as I looked at the suctioning apparatus that was hanging behind the bed.

It was 5:30 p.m. when we left Mel at Shock Trauma. His discharge orders were completed since noon, but we had to wait all day for the go-ahead. Betsy, his nurse that day, finally told us the transport to take Mel from Shock Trauma to Kernan was on its way.

Gathering a ridiculous amount of stuff that had accumulated in my "office" behind Mel's bed, Shana and I bagged the junk and lugged most of it home, where we went to eat a quick dinner with Moshe and Akiva.

I packed a small overnight bag and carefully followed the GPS directions to Kernan, a short half-hour drive from home. We wanted to get there before Mel did, but we could never have guessed that we had more than seven hours lead time.

Shana and I talked for a while, then turned our chairs around and faced away from the bed as I turned on the TV with the remote Shana found hanging off the side of the bed. We stared at the screen, waiting and worrying together.

Shana called home and spoke to Moshe.

"Is Akiva asleep?" she asked.

"Not yet," must have been his reply.

"Does he want to say good-night to me?"

"Hi Kivs, are you getting ready for bed? I'll be home soon. Be good for Abba, and I'll see you in the morning. I love you. Sleep tight, baby."

"Tell him Savta loves him, too," I added from the sidelines, wishing that we, Mel included, were home putting our precious grandson to bed.

Everyone's life was being uprooted by the accident. Shana and Moshe dropped everything – school, work and their lives in Israel – to be with us. Akiva probably didn't know what to make of this strange visit to his grandparents' home, especially since we were not where we belonged, hanging out with him. Becca and Simcha left work multiple times, taking time off they didn't really have to spare, pulling their kids from school and daycare, coming and going as often as they could, feeling the constant pull to be with us. Yael came back and forth from College Park amidst finals and final projects, wreaking havoc on her school and work schedule. To top it off, both Becca and Shana were pregnant, and these long days in the hospital were certainly taking an emotional and physical toll at a time when they were already exhausted.

I looked over at Shana, our calm, unflappable middle daughter, and she smiled at me. "It's all right, Mom," she said, reading my mind. "Akiva is happy with Moshe. I'll put him to bed tomorrow."

Moshe was doing a fantastic job keeping Akiva happy and occupied during this strange trip. As our chief home front support, he made sure that Shana got to and from the hospital, had meals ready when she came home and most importantly, gave her the emotional support I knew she needed during this crazy difficult time. I also knew how much he wanted to spend time with Mel, but he gave that time to Shana, understanding that she needed to be with her Abba.

At 9 o'clock I went back to the unit desk and asked if there was any news. "On his way," was the answer. At 9:30, I sent an exhausted, pregnant Shana home to rest. My heart didn't stop pounding until she called to let me know that she made it safely home. Of course, her cell had died earlier and I'm still not sure how she figured out the directions without a

GPS or cell phone. It was now approaching 11 o'clock. I trekked back to the unit desk. "Do you have any news for me?" I asked again.

The receptionist called dispatch again, "Still on the way. He should be here soon," she replied.

"Oh," I said wearily. "I'm really getting worried. Do you think he's okay? It's been hours and hours. What do you think is the holdup?"

"They didn't say that there was any issue. He should be here soon."

"I'm planning on staying over tonight, is that all right?"

"Of course. I'll look around and see if I can find a chair that reclines for you."

"That would be great, thanks," I said, managing a withered smile.

The night wore on. Nerves jangling, I lay down on my chaise and continued my vigil. Finally, at one in the morning, the transport team rolled Mel into the room. One look at his face and I was awake and fully alert.

"What happened?" I asked them.

"Nothing. It just took time," one replied as they transferred Mel to the bed.

It didn't look like nothing to me. Mel's face was green, haggard and certainly not fine. Mel waited until the men left the room. Shaking my head as I moved close to him, I bent down to hear him as he explained breathlessly.

"I was facing backward in the van," he gulped, "and we hit every pothole in the city! Every one!"

"Oh no!"

"I was sure that I was going to throw up. I almost did over and over. It took forever. It was torture!" He paused, breathing in and out with effort.

"And," he continued, not sure I could stomach much more. "They stopped all my pain meds at noon when the discharge orders came in. Betsy said they couldn't give me anything since then."

"Oh no, honey!" I exclaimed, tears shimmering in my eyes. I couldn't imagine how much pain he was in, having to go so many hours without medication in his condition. That is completely not okay, I thought, heading toward the door. "I'll be right back with the nurse. I'm going to get you some meds."

I met the nurse at the door. "Mel needs pain medication right away," I said. "He hasn't had anything for thirteen hours!"

"We can't get him any medication until the admitting doctor checks him over," she said to Mel.

"But it's been thirteen hours! He's in so much pain. The ride was horrible and made him sick," I persisted.

"Those are the rules. The doctor will be in soon."

"But," I stammered, "he's exhausted and hurting. Can't you do anything?"

"No. We have to wait for the doctor."

"Can I be suctioned?" Mel asked quietly, interrupting our banter.

"Yes," the nurse answered as she gathered the suction equipment from behind Mel's bed. Suctioning as well as respiratory treatments are routine and necessary for tracheostomy care. The upper airway warms, cleans and moistens the air we breathe. The trach tube bypasses these mechanisms, so that the air moving through the tube is cooler, dryer and not as clean. In response to these changes, the body produces more mucus[5]. As the mucus builds up, it

---

[5] http://www.hopkinsmedicine.org/tracheostomy/living/suctioning.html

must be cleared. Mel's upper respiratory muscles were still not strong enough to expel the mucus effectively.

The nurse removed Mel's speaking valve and proceeded with the suctioning. After a few seconds, she stopped. Mel indicated by pointing that he needed more. "He needs more," I said for him.

"We don't do that here," she stated.

"What do you mean?" I asked. "He needs more."

"Just this one time. We don't do repeated suctioning here."

Mel's pain-filled, frantic eyes met my incredulous, determined ones. We were not in Kansas anymore. Betsy had warned us things would be different. Was this what she meant? Carefully watching the nurse's every move, I took mental notes, learning instantly what I needed to do. Mel's needs would not be denied if I had anything to do with it. I perfected my suctioning skills over the next few days.

A long fraught-filled half-hour later, the admitting doctor arrived. Pain and sleep medications were prescribed and brought to Mel quickly. Various IV drips were started. Although the nurses came in throughout the night, we both managed a few hours of sleep, Mel's medically induced and mine exhaustion induced.

***

The morning came quickly, bringing footsteps to my chair. Blinking my eyes open, a warm smile greeted me.

"Hi, I'm Dr. J., the Chief Executive Officer here at Kernan. I wanted to welcome you and Mel personally."

I jumped up, now fully awake. Glancing at Mel's sleeping form, I led Dr. J. to the hallway trying desperately not to think about my wrinkled tee shirt, sloppy sweatpants, unsightly hair and the fact that we were speaking in close proximity, and I hadn't even found my toothbrush in my overnight bag.

"Thank you so much, Doctor. It is wonderful to meet you."

"We hope that Mel will make great progress here. I want you to know that I'm here if you need me for anything."

I knew that a few well-connected friends made calls on Mel's behalf, and I quickly decided that this impromptu visit was probably an expression of that interest, and I was glad.

Mel and I had once travelled first class on a trip to Israel. Two years earlier, within days of each other, Becca and Shana had both informed us that they were pregnant, Becca with her second child and Shana with her first. How to be in New Jersey and Israel at the same time was the question of the year, their due dates just nine days apart. Wanting to be with both of them, we waited anxiously without making any reservations. The stars shined on us; Becca delivered our beautiful granddaughter Eliora on August 4, and we were fortunate to spend a long wonderful weekend with her, Simcha and the girls. Shana was still holding on, so we set our travel agent to work. Cobbling together our various air reward points, she arranged an unexpected first class trip to Israel in time for Shana to deliver our handsome first grandson, Akiva, on August 18. The airline sported pod-shaped first class accommodations – I can't call them seats – they were so much more. Awestruck by the arrangement, my oohs of surprise prompted Mel to shake his head and say repeatedly, "Judy, just try to act as if you belong." Although experiencing the pods was lots of fun, it really wasn't in sync with my personality, and I contentedly went back to coach for the next leg of the trip.

So with great surprise, I realized that this special treatment was not only all right with me but sincerely welcomed. Having the CEO greet us first thing in the morning of our first day was very special indeed. In this case, unlike on the plane, I was all for anything that would help Mel be more comfortable and progress to his fullest potential. Our many thanks to Dr. J., who did follow our progress and to whom we did turn to on various occasions, as well as to the friends behind the scenes who made this happen. Although we had a rough start at Kernan, something I did mention to Dr. J., the therapist and support staff were excellent, and they made all the difference. Mel's private corner room wasn't too bad either.

***

Mel's first day at Kernan was busy with assessments. Lauren, an exuberant, ponytailed, brunette OT, appeared early in the morning, not long after Dr. J. left. Mel's fingers, hands and arms were evaluated for muscle strength. Lauren quickly tested them by applying pressure to each body part and having Mel press back. She then jotted down a value from zero to five for each muscle group. Zero indicated no movement or response; five indicated normal range. Mel had only one score that was close to normal, his left bicep. His scores showed us that an enormous amount of recovery was needed.

In the afternoon we met Beth, Mel's PT. Young and vibrant, Beth exuded confidence. It would be Beth's job to rebuild Mel. She too evaluated Mel's muscles using a zero to five scale. Beth assessed all the major muscle groups of his body. Again the scores were very low, the work ahead daunting.

"Tomorrow, the real work begins," Beth said. "Get some rest."

Day 19

May 22, 2013

Mel's first day of rehab was grueling. The transport didn't arrive until after 11p.m. and intake ran until 1am. Exhausted, Mel had assessments in speech therapy, occupational therapy, physical therapy as well as various additional assessments by doctors and the dietician. Each person said that the work begins tomorrow. Please continue to daven for him to find the strength to do all he needs to do and handle all he must handle.

Day 20

May 23, 2013

Today Mel's real work began. He had two full hours of occupational therapy and a full hour of physical therapy. You will not be surprised to hear that Beth, Mel's PT, said she was going to have to watch out because Mel was already doing so well that the other PTs would want to steal him from her. The move to rehab has already made such a difference! It was awesome to wheel him outside, dressed in real clothes, and watch him interacting with our little grandson, Akiva. Baruch HaShem.

Healing Garden

"Do you want to look around and see this place?" I asked Mel after his morning OT therapy session later that week.

"Sure. I want to practice driving this thing," he said referring to his automatic wheelchair.

We would later learn the endless possibilities in wheelchair adaptation based on individual needs, but for that moment Mel was happy to try out the new long toggle-type adaptive device on the control which Lauren had just connected during his therapy session. The hope was that Mel would find this type of control mechanism more effective for his limited finger strength and range of motion, of which he had virtually none. Instead, he could utilize the side of his hand rather than his fingers which he could do with much greater effectiveness.

I gathered my backpack as I moved the tray table out of the way. After I maneuvered the wheelchair toward the door, Mel was off. Within moments, we could see the huge benefit of the control device. Down the long straight hallway to the elevators we went. I pushed the button, Mel advanced into the elevator with me following close behind. The building wasn't really that complicated or large. There were two primary levels with four units of rehabilitation: spinal cord injury, orthopedic and medical injury, brain injury and stroke. Therapy gyms, patient rooms and offices made up most of the rest of the space.

We followed the main drag down a somewhat steep decline, and I was hugely relieved that the chair was automatic. It was there that we found a real jewel adjacent to the cafeteria.

Nestled off the far end of the lower level was a carefully tended healing garden. Flowing gradually downhill, we saw blossoming flowers, shrubs, small trees and wooden benches placed strategically throughout to sit and enjoy the peaceful atmosphere. A small wooden bridge overlooked the quiet, serene grounds. It was to this outside oasis that Mel and I would often escape. It was a gift to us; a few moments of relative privacy and space for our thoughts, a break from the relentless awful reality we were living.

We made our way toward a bench under a small tree, not far down the path. That spot became my favorite place at Kernan. Mel stopped the wheelchair beside the bench, and I locked the brake then sat down on the bench close to Mel's chair. I felt so much give way inside of me as Mel and I took in the beauty that surrounded us. I think he felt that as well, as he leaned the chair back into a pressure-release, changing from his upright position in order to prevent pressure sores. All of Mel's therapists made sure to allow adequate time and opportunity for pressure-releases during their sessions, and I noticed that the patients took advantage.

As he released back we sat together quietly. It felt heavenly – almost surreal – to be outside together on that beautiful early summer day, the sun on our faces, warmth and nature surrounding us. The wonder of having Mel to myself and feeling like a couple out on our own was heady. The intimacy and beauty of that time was hard to leave, and it made me somewhat irresponsible. I let it continue for at least half an hour.

Forcing ourselves to return to "real life," we made our way back the way we had come and were in Mel's room not 45 minutes from the time we left.

"Where have you been?" his nurse of the day demanded bearing down on us as we entered the room.

"We went to the healing garden. It was so beautiful there."

"Well, I had his medicine and couldn't find him to give it to him," she reprimanded.

"Oh. I'm so sorry," I stuttered. "Is it too late now?"

"Not really," she said. "I'll get it for him. You wait here," she said stressing the word here.

"Could you please bring it to the therapy gym? We should be going there shortly," I said timidly.

"Next time, be here," she replied.

Uh-oh, I thought. We've done it now.

"I thought it was all right to leave since you didn't have afternoon therapy for over an hour," I said to Mel, shrugging. "We should be more careful."

"It's okay," he said. "I can take the medicine now. We weren't gone that long."

Noticing the pinkish hue on his nose and cheeks, I felt even guiltier. "It was nice out there wasn't it?" Mel said.

"Yes. It really was," I replied. "Let's go back soon. We'll tell someone when we go."

"Deal."

***

Mel's inpatient days were busy and structured with Occupational Therapy every morning at 9:30 and Physical Therapy every afternoon at 1:00. Each session was an hour long and was done on a one-on-one basis, except for Saturdays. The support Mel received from our community was nothing short of incredible, and I received a daily barrage of requests to visit. It was beautiful and heartwarming, and I had a difficult time saying no. The therapy was grueling, and Mel needed his strength for the work. I did severely limit the number of visitors, although by late afternoon, I found that he could handle and even looked forward to short visits.

Our core group was there constantly, cheering and providing us with whatever they could do.

Sherri brought a special cozy blanket for my cot. Each Friday she came by Mel's room, prepared my bed for me while I was home taking a shower and then left a candy on my pillow with a note.

"There isn't enough food for Shabbat. Mel is finally eating and I'm not sure we have enough," I called Pam in a panic.

"I'll be there soon," she said. Barely half an hour later, she walked in with enough food for an army.

Pam's husband, Neil, works long hours as a psychologist. His difficult schedule did not allow him to visit during the daytime. Instead, he spent many an evening with his friend Mel watching ball games and keeping the nighttime terrors at bay a bit longer.

When I excitedly told Malki, our amazing *Bikur Cholim* coordinator, that Mel was able to swallow fluids, she appeared two hours later with several containers of her mother's famous chicken soup. Mel and I still talk about how delicious it was. This was in addition to the constant organization of all our food needs for months.

Gary, our home accessibility guru, found us chair rails and organized their installation for our difficult split-level house configuration. A beautiful wooden ramp was commissioned and built in a matter of days because Gary knew how to get the job done. The building theme continued when Gary gave Mel a brand new improved smile with his dental expertise. No more gaping hole where Mel's front middle tooth once resided, no more crooked incisors from a youthful botched orthodontic endeavor. Only perfection from our Gary.

Our eleven-year-old niece Michal cheered her uncle up each time she visited with her bright smile and home-made cards and gifts. A striped teddy bear was Mel's favorite.

Although our situation was far from optimal, Larry's legal advice and expertise made all the difference.

Michael and Marci appeared at the most opportune moments. It seemed they had a sixth sense of when something unique or weird was needed. They were the ones we sent for batteries and fish cakes. Who knew those things could be a necessity?

Our longtime family friends Barbara and Howard and my brother Harry and sister-in-law Shelley visited us when no one else could, embodying the true meaning and intent of visiting the sick. They genuinely helped us manage through the most difficult time of each week. We will never forget their kindness.

The range of good deeds, thoughts and actions by those around us and on our behalf was awe-inspiring. These are but a few, a taste of the love and goodness that exist in our world.

Florence Nightingale

Nurse Nicole walked into Mel's hospital room and into his life during his first week at Kernan. With light brown shoulder-length hair, medium stature, efficient manner and effervescent personality, Nicole was the first caretaker to really see past Mel's broken outer trappings to the brilliant jewel that is my husband. The connection between them was instantaneous, and I could have even felt a pang of jealousy if it weren't for the fact that Nicole was there to provide the essential ingredient missing from Mel's rehabilitation up until now. Here was someone completely new to Mel, someone with no past association with pre-injury Mel: a new friend. A born extrovert, Mel truly enjoys every aspect of being with people: talking, getting involved with personal projects, helping and being a great friend to all. Nicole is a kindred spirit. She would pop into Mel's room for a few minutes each night just to visit. I think Mel's happiest nights at Kernan were those few when she was his nurse. We felt like we hit the jackpot when she was assigned to Mel's care during those first few weeks when he could barely move a muscle. Whether this was an intentional part of Mel's care plan or just pure luck, we will never know.

What we do know is that Nicole was Mel's special angel, sent to bring out his shining spirit, the essence that was submerged beneath a traumatized exterior. She accomplished this with genuine kindness, honesty and a good deal of laughter. She saw Mel, the real Mel, with fresh eyes and an open heart. Of course, anyone who knew Mel before the accident also knew what lay underneath his nearly-paralyzed exterior, but it was Nicole who convinced him that his essence was still very much a part of him, and evident even to a new acquaintance like her. He was still able to make friends, that part of him still blessedly intact.

Dysphagia II

I pushed Mel in his wheelchair to the other end of the main hallway, the side farthest from his hospital room, to a tiny office for his second swallow test, the disappointment of the first fresh in our minds. He was given small amounts of thin liquids and then thicker fluids and soft foods like mashed up graham crackers and pudding. Then imaging was used to determine whether the fluid or food followed the correct pathway down his esophagus.

I was asked to wait outside. Two closed doors and three folding chairs filled the space. The walls were white and nondescript. Hunched over, I could not check the tears that flowed down my face as I looked over at the one other person waiting in the hallway. "Please God, please help him to pass this test. He is so very thirsty. Please allow him to have a Slurpee," I prayed over and over.

Within minutes, the door opened and Mel's speech therapist motioned me in to the room. The mood was somber; Mel had not passed. "He's not ready yet," she said. "We'll try again next week."

It was so cruel, so unfair, yet Mel would need to wait. His body was not strong enough. His eyes were full of pain. I held my own sadness in check as I pushed him back to his room, the wheels on the floor the only sound. What would we do? The only thing we could do. Keep on going.

Heartbreak

To entertain my visiting grandchildren during those long summer days, I borrowed a sprinkler from the young family who lived next door. It slithered along our front lawn, spraying water in small arcs. I watched Shira and Eliora run in and out of the sprinkler, adorable in their pink and purple bathing suits. Akiva was shy and hovered near Shana as the girls squealed. Smiling, I called him to me.

"Sit on my lap, Kivs. We'll watch the girls together."

Sitting in lawn chairs on the edge of the driveway with Becca, Shana, and Akiva, I was actually able to enjoy a few moments of relative normalcy. Simcha was out for a run and Moshe was busy indoors.

I had left Mel in the care of his nurses for a few hours in order to make my way home, rest a bit, shower and prepare for Shabbat. I looked from precious face to precious face and wished the clock would stop.

But it did not.

Before I knew it I was kissing the kids goodbye. Unfortunately, there were no hotels near Kernan, and no place for the family to stay with us over Shabbat. It's a rare occurrence for our children to be together in the same place at the same time, yet that Shabbat they would be under one roof. It was inconceivable that Mel and I would not be with them. Kernan was less than ten miles away, but for us the expanse felt like an ocean.

After saying goodbye, I got in the car and couldn't resist looking back as I headed to the cross street. Three little faces at the window tore at my heart. I waved and sent air kisses as my tears began to flow. Life's unfairness nearly overpowered me. All I wanted was for my family to be together, the stuff of dreams in my present reality.

I turned the corner and headed to Mel, sniffling the rest of the way.

Kiddush Cup #1

As a *Baalat Teshuva,* I came to an understanding of Shabbat in my late teens. A random question from an unlikely source spurred me to celebrate my first Shabbat and I have been profoundly changed by its weekly observance ever since. The spiritual change from weekday to Shabbat is palpable, created by including special practices and refraining from others. The opportunity for rest, renewal and reconnection with loved ones, community and God each week is a perpetual gift.

It never occurred to me that this could be taken away. Shabbat was something I chose to embrace, and it would be there for me each week, like the setting of the sun. When Mel was an inpatient at Kernan, I felt that Shabbat was taken from us. Our world was now the world of Kernan Hospital, a completely secular environment where spirituality was needed to get you through, but the trappings of religion had no place.

For that first Shabbat, Pam arranged meals by enlisting the help of our generous community. She then plated the food for me to simplify the preparation, a beautiful and thoughtful gesture. The donated refrigerator was generously stocked. At this point Mel was still on a feeding tube and having failed the swallow test the week before, was unable to drink. Not even a swallow of water was permitted.

Miserably, I heated my platter of food in the communal eating area and brought it to Mel's room. He watched me light the electric Shabbat candles and listened as I made the appropriate blessing over them, ushering in our first Shabbat at Kernan and the third since the accident. It was nice to have the electric candelabra, a welcome step up from turning on the light switch, my method for the previous two Fridays. It was comforting to say the *bracha* again rather than my banal declaration that it was Shabbat. Along with the food, Pam had lovingly included a package of fancy plastic wine goblets made to resemble silver kiddush cups, the special cups used for blessing the wine at the start of Shabbat and holiday meals. It was a pack of ten. As I pulled the first one apart from the others, I wondered if we would still be in Kernan for the tenth and final cup. Would we need another package?

Mel and I had been married for almost 29 years. In all that time we had been apart only a handful of *Shabbatot* and rarely did I have to recite the Kiddush blessings. Mel was able to speak with the mouthpiece over his trach tube but he was unable to drink the grape juice. Pouring the juice to the top of the cup, I turned to him, propped up to a nearly seated position. Mel looked at me expectantly through his clear blue eyes.

"Are you ready to hear Kiddush?" I asked quietly.

"Yes, go ahead," he replied as we both looked away and tried not to sulk. I picked up the prayer book and found the correct page.

"You are with me and that's amazing," I said catching his gaze once again before beginning. I lifted the cup and slowly recited the words that Mel had recited thousands of times in over 1500 *Shabbatot* we had shared.

"It's all right," he said noticing my hesitation to drink the juice, the final part of the ritual. No liquid passed his lips in the three weeks since the accident. His need to drink, to feel the fluid flow down and soothe his battered throat and quench a nearly insatiable thirst was something he thought about constantly. It had become his most fervent need. He didn't need to voice it; the look in his eyes when he was allowed a meager ice chip spoke volumes. I had stopped drinking in his presence. It was too cruel. The simple Kiddush service and the delicious grape juice, something I always looked forward to drinking and enjoyed so much, had turned into a trial, a test.

I turned my back and choked down the juice, nearly emptying the cup in order to fulfill the commandment according to tradition.

"You did a good job," Mel said encouragingly. "Go eat your dinner. You must be hungry."

Now I had to eat. This was a sickening new reality. Eat and drink in front of the person dearest to you who cannot. How could I eat a morsel when Mel couldn't eat? How could I do so in front of him? I offered to take the food elsewhere, but he asked me to stay. I placed my plate of food on the counter next to the sink in the room. There was a curtain that could be drawn for privacy, shielding the bed from the door. As Mel closed his eyes to rest, I pulled the curtain and positioned my chair and plate on the far end of the counter behind it. As quietly as possible, I washed my hands in the sink, gathered two rolls, made the blessing over them and forced down a bite. I sat down on the high stool by the counter and ate a small amount of the hefty portion. I am sure the food was delicious, prepared and plated with love, but honestly it was impossible to taste with any enjoyment.

Our first Shabbat at Kernan had begun.

Mel's night nurse came in and noticed my dinner arrangement. She didn't say a word as she opened the curtain to bring Mel his evening meds, which included painkillers and Ambien. This was a good thing, for sleep is something he needed to escape the nightmarish reality for a few hours.

I wrapped my mostly uneaten plate of food and put it in the refrigerator. Of course, it would eventually be thrown out since the refrigerator was bulging with generosity from our friends and community. I simply couldn't handle any more guilt at the moment by throwing out good food. I slipped quietly into the bathroom and changed into a tee shirt and sweatpants, and made my way to the fold-down chair next to Mel's bed. He was starting to doze off, so as quietly as possible I arranged the sheet and blanket that the nurse had left for me at my request and settled in. It was surprisingly comfortable, or maybe I was just too exhausted to notice that it wasn't.

"Do you want me to take off the speaking valve now?" I asked Mel. The staff did not want the valve on overnight. They felt it was more difficult to breathe through it, although Mel claimed he felt no difference in his breathing with it on or off. Regardless, he was compliant. In fact, I learned that Mel is an extremely compliant patient. He listens to the rules and rarely questions them. Not that he is a follower. On the contrary, he is actually a strong leader who believes in a structure and guidelines and the order of things. He follows the rules. We have that in common.

"Yes," he answered.

"Is the medication starting to work?" I asked.

"I think so, thank God," he answered.

I got up and moved closer to Mel. I carefully removed the valve, sorry to see it go. I was his voice for the night.

"I love you, Mel," I said.

I love you, too, he mouthed.

I arranged his blanket over his chest and went back to my makeshift bed and settled in for my nightly series of naps. Mel needed to be turned every two hours to make sure he didn't develop bedsores. Each turn was a complicated process because it was extremely difficult for Mel to get comfortable. The neck brace, which he had to wear for twelve full weeks, limited how he could be rolled from side to side. Heavy booties with small kickstand-like levers on each side were placed on Mel's feet each night to prevent problems with his ankles and with toe dropping. His hands were similarly immobilized inside big mittens.

The positioning began with the aide lowering the head of the bed until Mel was lying completely flat. While standing on one side of the bed, the aide would pull the top sheet underneath Mel while simultaneously lifting, causing Mel to roll away from the aide partially onto his side. The aide would then bend Mel's legs and position one on top of or in front of the other, open the kickstands to support the feet and keep them at a healthy angle. Finally, the positioning of Mel's neck would ensue. This could take many attempts and force the aide to begin the whole process again. It involved rolling one or two pillows under his neck and head. The angle was very important, because if the pillows were set incorrectly, the neck brace would become unbearable. Mel tried to remain patient throughout the process, but by the time he was marginally comfortable, his patience would often be sorely tried. It was heartbreaking to watch, but I did watch and very carefully noted the angle of his shoulders and neck, and pillow height – even which colored pillows were most comfortable.

The whole procedure was physically and emotionally draining. He couldn't move any limbs at this point. He couldn't adjust himself in any way without assistance. But things were a bit better – this week he could speak through the valve and tell us what he needed. I was grateful for that and held onto his ability to communicate like a lifeline. As the weeks progressed, Mel was able to make small movements and help with the adjustments as needed.

Day 22

May 25, 2013

I didn't write before Shabbat, because I often wait for the moment each day that speaks to me. That poignant moment came right before Shabbat when Mel, using his new mastery over the speaking valve on his trach, was able to clearly give Shabbat brachot to our daughters.

With sincere gratitude to Hashem, Mel is improving every day and his attitude continues to be upbeat. Although many people wish to visit, please please refrain from coming to visit for a while longer. We greatly appreciate all the love and support that so many have demonstrated toward us, but the therapy is exhausting and his energy is limited.

Don't Be Sick on Saturday

Waking up the first Saturday morning at Kernan, we could already feel the different, slower vibe here compared to the fast pace in the hospital. The halls were quieter and the nurses' aides came in to help Mel with his morning preparations much later. We were glad his first therapy wasn't scheduled until 11 a.m.

We quickly realized that the staff was pared down and getting help would be a challenge. It had only been less than a week since Mel's discharge from Shock Trauma and he was still attached to his tracheostomy tube. His sats had leveled out and he had been doing beautifully all week. After the tumult of dressing and a harrowing transfer to his wheelchair, we both needed a rest. Pulling up a chair beside him in his room, I sat quietly with him and together we waited until 11 a.m. for his first therapy session.

"I'm not feeling so good," he told me, breathing hard.

Concerned, I watched him for a full minute. "Try to relax," I cautioned. "I'll go find the nurse."

Heading into the hallway, I looked around and spotted a nurse far up the corridor. I intercepted her just as she was turning the corner.

"My husband doesn't feel well. Would you please come and check on him?" I asked.

"I'll be in soon," she responded.

Quickly, I made my way back to Mel. "She'll be right here," I told him.

He was still breathing with difficulty, but he was breathing. Nervously, I stood by the door waiting for the nurse, and after several minutes I went out to look for her. Mel was still winded. Spotting the nurse as she emerged from another patient's room, I approached her again.

"Mel is really winded, please come check on him," I pleaded.

She followed me into the room, briefly glanced at Mel and started scanning the room. Not finding an oxygen saturation monitor, she went to look for one and retuned a few minutes later with the device. She attached it to Mel's forefinger as we waited. Sure enough, Mel's oxygen level was a bit low, although thankfully not dangerously low.

"He could use some oxygen," she said. "Where's his oxygen tank?"

Mel and I looked at each other. I shrugged. "I don't know. I don't think he has one," I replied.

"Well, he needs to have one with his wheelchair. Isn't he going to therapy? He needs to take one with him."

Again, I shrugged, thinking that we certainly didn't know that he needed one. This was news, since he hadn't had one all week.

"I'll go find one for him. He needs it before he goes off to therapy," she said.

I sat down next to Mel and we looked at each other. I watched him breathe for many labored breaths. Surely we were not in Kansas anymore. Betsy's words rang in my ears, "It's really different there," she had told us about Kernan versus Shock Trauma, "you need to prepare yourselves." We didn't understand what she meant at the time, but it was becoming clear to us now. Kernan was an amazing place for therapy and rehabilitation, but the nursing care was simply not the same. We had to be on our toes, advocate for ourselves and keep up with everything. If I had known where to get an oxygen tank I would have run to get it, but since I wasn't yet familiar with our new surroundings I stayed put, watching Mel, checking the clock repeatedly, and wringing my hands.

Mel's breathing suddenly became less labored. "I feel better," he said.

Relieved, I started busying myself around the room, straightening our growing collection of stuff. Then I moved to the refrigerator and fiddled with assorted containers, moving things around just for the sake of having something to do, a way of letting out my frustration.

The nurse rushed back into Mel's room lugging an oxygen tank. Approaching Mel's chair back, she asked, "Where is his strap for the oxygen?"

"We don't think he has one. We don't think he ever had an oxygen tank," I replied, looking to Mel for confirmation.

"Well, he needs a strap," she said with annoyance. Then she rushed out again.

"I'm sure glad you fixed yourself," I told Mel.

He gave me a half smile. "I guess I'll manage without the oxygen."

I nodded. "Yeah, it's a good thing."

Checking the clock above the refrigerator, I said, "It's time for therapy. Let's go." As I rolled Mel down the hall to therapy the nurse stopped us midway, strap in hand.

"Wait a minute. We need to connect the oxygen tank," she spluttered. Rolling our eyes, we stopped and let her affix the tank. By then, Mel was late for therapy and we were both truly annoyed. Mel never used the oxygen that day or any other day for that matter. Surprisingly, this was the one and only day that we asked for oxygen and the only time he had an oxygen tank on the back of his wheelchair.

Finally, we made our way to the gym and Mel's morning OT therapy. The gym was a sight to see on that first Saturday.

Always a hive of activity, it was humming with a busy feeling different than the weekdays. Instead of individual one-on-one therapy, we saw group therapy with one or two therapists helping many patients. As we entered the cheerfully colored gym, we saw a long row of patients along the right side of the gym in various stages of recovery in wheelchairs and in regular chairs waiting for their turns to do the group walking activity. As we moved farther into the brightly lit space, we saw patients clustered around a few therapists working on strengthening exercises. The side of the gym closest to Mel's room was for Physical Therapy and the side farthest for Occupational Therapy as well as Outpatient Therapy.

We were approached by a therapist who motioned us to the far right corner of the room where Mel's group was gathering. Animated voices, laughter, moans, clanging of equipment and sounds of productive activity filled the air. The gym was a good place where real work happened and real recovery was achieved; the energy was palpable, vibrant and positive. Mel joined a group of four men in powered wheelchairs.

Male Sexuality

Once our small group assembled, we were ushered into a tiny office located in the far corner of the gym. One of the therapists loaded a DVD into a DVD player connected to the TV and announced the day's topic: Male Sexuality.

I looked up from my seat on the therapy practice bed crammed closely behind Mel's wheelchair and asked, "Should I be here?"

"Yes. Of course," she replied. "This very much involves you too."

I nodded in recognition of her answer but my facial expression was definitely telling another story altogether.

On the previous Shabbat, just seven days before, Mel was in Shock Trauma doing a tracheostomy trial and fighting to breathe on his own. I didn't see that sex was really next on our list of activities. I looked at Mel and realized he was not paying the least bit of attention. He was trying to get comfortable in the chair. He pressed the button to tilt the chair back and got settled into a pressure release. As he closed his eyes, I knew he was far away. I remained where I was. At least one of us should know whatever it is that they want us to know, I thought.

There must be a reason why they put us in this class on this particular day. Unfortunately for me, I didn't understand the system yet. There was an entire loose-leaf binder filled with information from all the classes they were required to offer to spinal cord patients. These classes ran based on staff availability and not necessarily on the appropriateness for the patient in the path of their recovery.

Mel slept, and I watched a tasteful but emotional documentary on male sexuality following a spinal cord injury. It explored the potential problems, the emotional and physical details, as well as methods to deal with the problems and find ways to live fulfilling intimate lives.

I watched, and Mel slept. I watched in a tiny room with four other men, minus the therapist who had stepped out once the movie began. It was Shabbat. I wasn't technically breaking the laws of Shabbat, but I was certainly breaking the spirit. I felt that I had no choice. I needed to gather any information available that would help Mel. So I watched while Mel slept.

Later, he didn't remember one second of the experience. I, on the other hand, was deeply disturbed by the whole thing. It was too soon for me to deal with this issue, let alone think about it. Why was this forced upon us/me now? It depressed me as nothing had up to this point and made me feel that the road ahead was too long, too painful, too unknown. I just didn't have the time or the strength for it.

I found myself complaining to the head nurse about the movie the following week as I explained that the topic had greatly upset me. I asked her what the reasoning was behind Mel's assignment to that particular class on that particular day. She listened and agreed with me and said that we could refuse to attend classes. She recommended that we ask in advance which sessions Mel was assigned to on the modified Saturday schedule and choose working/physical sessions.

"Wonderful," I replied. From then on, each Friday morning, when asked what type of sessions Mel wanted the following day, we chose the active working sessions.

I have a dear friend who teases me because I am a rule follower. Count on me to toe the line. It's a standing joke between us. To be honest, I am comfortable following the rules, and so is Mel. I believe that his adherence to and compliance with the rules truly made a difference in his recovery. But we do know when to draw the line, and attending the "informational" sessions at Kernan just didn't cut it. Like the Male Sexuality session, we felt they had the potential to overload us with unnecessary and untimely information. Instead, we researched, asked questions, found and reached out to experts in our knowledgeable and generous greater community, gathering our information as it was needed, in a way that worked for our specific case.

Routine

Our days were turbulent. Mel and I together and separately dealt with the ups and downs buffeted by the winds of challenges and uncertainty. As a caregiver, I found a lifeline in routine.

We humans like routines, and I believe we thrive on routine. It can of course have a negative connotation, but I discovered during this most trying time of my life that routine was crucial, some predictability essential, in order to deal with the madness of it all.

At the time of the accident and for years after, I taught a yoga class on Wednesday mornings at our local Jewish Community Center. The first Tuesday post-accident, I called my supervisor to tell her I would not be able to teach my class the following morning. Explaining our circumstances, she immediately asked if I wanted to suspend the classes until things calmed down.

"Let's not cancel it just yet," I said, knowing how much my students enjoyed the class and not wanting to give up on everything in my life. "Let's see what next week brings."

She agreed to give it a few weeks and quickly found a substitute for the next day.

Of course, I had no idea what the following weeks would bring. I could barely manage the next few minutes, but I did hope that I could keep something of my pre-accident life, some iota of my regular life routine. I felt that it was important for me, and because it was important to me, I made this one class, this one hour and fifteen minutes per week a priority for me. In retrospect, I am sure that by allowing myself to continue this one act, to find this much time for myself when there was really none, was a lifeline for me as a caregiver and advocate.

There were many nights when worry kept me up and wired, feeling guilty that I would get to Mel later than other days, unsure how I would physically make it through class, yet I rallied for that one small space of time. I was a normal person doing a normal activity. As it turns out, through the many weeks of Mel's recovery, I was able to carve out this one hour and fifteen minutes each week. Amazingly, I only missed the very first week. To boot, I found that my class did not suffer, because I dug deep and used the lessons I was learning, watching and being part of Mel's miraculous recovery, to provide inspiration for my classes. Complimenting me on a beautiful class, a daughter of one of my regular students who attended during this time expressed her surprise when her mother told her that I was going through such a difficult time. "I would never have known!" she said. "You are so calm and in control."

Focusing on my class, forcing my mind and attention on something other than the crisis, gave me a much-needed mental rest. Getting to do yoga once a week wasn't bad either. Afterward, I was able to drive the short distance to the hospitals feeling renewed. Having a few minutes, a time that I knew would come each week, was an anchor for me. Maintaining one small slice of my life allowed me to feel connected to that life. All was not lost.

The days were long, exhausting and often overwhelming. In the first weeks, I arrived at Shock Trauma by 8:30, in time for rounds. Sitting by Mel's side, speaking with doctors and therapists, helping him to communicate, moving Mel's arms and legs for our own PT sessions, watching Mel's monitors for anything untoward, reading him the CaringBridge entries and comments, these were the activities of the day. I even acted as bodyguard and gatekeeper, monitoring his visitors and keeping most out.

One time, a kind and caring rabbi from our community who knew Mel personally appeared at Mel's doorway in Shock Trauma. Unfortunately, I did not know who he was, but I don't think this would have changed the outcome. He came to Shock Trauma to visit Mel. I met him at the curtain to Mel's room and nicely but firmly explained that Mel was not up to visitors. Sadly, he turned away. Three months later, he tried again, this time visiting our home. Mel ushered him in and introduced us properly. "Your wife was quite the guard," he said. "She was actually a little scary." Me scary? To anyone who knows me this seems impossible, yet at that time perhaps I was.

Each night I waited for the night shift to begin in earnest so I could speak to the night nurse. Understandably, this was often an extremely agitated time for Mel. The nurses at Shock Trauma were amazing as a whole, but Mel had experienced one particularly terrifying night and I couldn't chance a repeat.

It was early on, the first week post-accident, and Mel was having grave difficulty with his intubation. I think it may even have been the night of the failed extubation. I left him as usual after meeting the night nurse. We discussed Mel's difficulty breathing and his need for frequent suctioning. We discussed Mel's near paralysis, his only moveable appendage being his left arm which he could lift slightly with great effort. This was his only way to signal for help. I stressed how vulnerable and how uncomfortable he was. After confirming all this with the nurse and then relaying our words to Mel, I kissed him goodnight and went home. It was only Karen's words to me, the need for my strength for the long haul, which propelled me out that door and into the car headed home. At 11 p.m. I called the nurses' station and spoke to Mel's nurse, reiterating my earlier statements. Assuring me that all was well, he failed to heed any of my instructions or pay attention to any of Mel's needs.

I found Mel distraught the next morning. Letter by letter, I slowly learned that the nurse had not been looking through the glass at Mel during the night. Mel had signaled repeatedly for help, lifting his weary arm as high as he could over and over and over while choking on the secretions in his throat. He needed suctioning desperately, and he felt that he would drown. Once I calmed Mel and myself down enough to speak to anyone, I had some words with the head nurse. Needless to say, the night nurse from that appalling evening was never assigned to him again.

From then on, each night I waited to speak to Mel's night nurse to make sure that it was not the offending nurse. The days were endless, and I left the hospital bone-tired. But each night I had a small routine that helped me through. As soon as I walked in the door, I would leave my shoes by the front door, and then I would take a shower to wash off any vestiges of the hospital. My clothes went right in the hamper. If I had not completed my CaringBridge entry, I would sit myself down munching on a snack and write it, sending it off to cyberspace with a prayer that my words would help Mel. Just before 11, I would make my call to the hospital and check on Mel. Was he resting? How were the past two hours? Then I would lie down on the bed, cover up and watch *Everybody Loves Raymond*, a sitcom I had never watched prior to the accident. Nestled into the 11-11:30 p.m. slot, I had happened upon the show during the first week. Alone in our room where my tears threatened, knowing that Mel was not coming home for the first time in 29 years, I spent a half hour each night letting the silliness wash over me, letting the coordinated laughter fill my ears with something I didn't hear much during those days. I let myself think about the ordinary problems of interfering mothers-in-law, husband and wife mishaps, and I even laughed out loud. In our certain segments of our community, television is seen as harmful. I understand the point of view. There is so much that is distasteful and bad on television. But at that time in my life, during the circumstances in which I found myself, a simple sitcom was not a bad thing because it allowed me a few moments of respite. It became an important part of my nightly routine.

My routine changed less than expected when Mel progressed to Kernan. Except for the first week when I slept in a cot by Mel's bed, I began the day and arrived around 8:30, in time to help him with breakfast and early grooming, and then we were off to OT at 9:30. I helped with the OT range of motion warmups, taking one hand while Lauren, his therapist, took the other. I mimicked her actions and learned the proper order and method of the warm-ups. This would free Lauren up to go further with Mel and accomplish more in the 45-minute session. The only day I did not make it for warm-ups was Wednesday, the day of my yoga class. I wouldn't let guilt stop me, although it was a challenge each week.

The evenings often ran a bit longer at Kernan. I would wait until Mel was settled in bed, some time after 9 p.m. Settled is the operative term. Finding a comfortable position, the perfect pillow height and spot was nearly impossible with the protruding, oppressive neck brace. The process of adjusting could go on for a seemingly endless length of time with Mel's frustration growing. Certain nursing aides were good at this task and others hopeless. I studied the pillows, the location and the angles, as if it were a board exam. I tried it myself, sometimes successfully, often failing miserably.

Once Mel was ready, often settling for a position that really would give him little ease, I would say my goodbye. My last duties before leaving him for the night were laying out his clothes for the next day and closing the corner window shades; signals that this day was on the books.

At home, my routine remained the same; shoes at the door, shower, CaringBridge and snack, phone call, sitcom and then lights out. I found comfort in the predictability.

Vision Woes

Mel has been wearing glasses since the third grade. He was not particularly comfortable with the idea of touching his eyes, so his adjustment to contacts was slow and awkward at age 30. It took him weeks to get over his squeamishness, but once he did, he was sold. So rarely does anyone but me see him in glasses. I really like the look.

Once I told the nurse that Mel was wearing his contacts during surgery, they were removed, but he had nothing with which to replace them. Mel's nearsightedness was far from a priority for his medical team and it wasn't on my radar either. This was not so for Mel. He managed, day in and day out, to see his crazy post-accident world through blurred eyes, which must have added another surreal dimension to his situation.

Nearly three weeks after surgery Mel finally said something about his vision.

"It would really help if I could see better. Could you bring my glasses or contacts from home?" he asked.

"Of course," I replied. "But I don't think I'll be able to put your contacts in for you." I only wore reading glasses and had no experience with contacts. "I'll try, but I don't know how it will go."

Realizing that Mel's fingers were not dexterous enough to manipulate contacts, I suggested that he start with his glasses. Unfortunately his eyesight had also taken a jolt from the accident, and his prescription had changed enough to make his glasses fairly useless.

So I called our friend and favorite optometrist, Chaim.

"I'll be by this afternoon," Chaim said immediately. "Tell him I'm on the way."

True to his word, Chaim showed up later that day with an eye chart and measuring tools. He conducted a complete vision test.

"Your prescription has changed quite a bit," he told Mel. "I'll bring by a new pair of glasses for you tomorrow."

Chaim came through with the glasses and a smile. As he positioned them on the bridge of Mel's nose, Mel's world slid into focus.

"You have a lot of admirers out there," he said pointing to Mel and brushing off any offers of payment. "A friend of mine made them for you. It's a gift."

Thanking Chaim and recognizing once again the goodness around us, Mel was now able to put his clearer vision to good use. His progress in and out of therapy improved with amazing speed.

Not more than two weeks later, Mel urged me to bring him contacts. I again called on Chaim who came to the hospital that very day with various sample lenses and found a suitable pair. Mel then began the arduous task of figuring out a method to insert and remove the lenses. This was no easy undertaking. Although Mel had made significant progress in the dexterity of his fingers, his right side continued to lag far behind the left. The absence of sensation in his fingertips didn't help either. Being right-handed, Mel was accustomed to using his right hand for most things, shooting and dribbling a basketball with his left being notable exceptions. But Mel was determined to get those contacts into his eyes. He spent hours putting in both the right and left lenses with his left hand, then created a crossover method that seemed to work well for him. I passed many of those hours searching for a clear round disc on the white tile floor of his hospital room, his shirt, and his wheelchair. Once it took me nearly a quarter of an hour to find it hanging off his cheek. Yet Mel was determined. Even when I pleaded for him to give it up for the day and try again tomorrow, Mel wouldn't stop trying. Frustration ruled but perseverance won out. He had accomplished this vital task himself and was moving toward independence, his vision and outlook markedly clearer.

As the months wore on, this task fell into the "I can do it almost as fast as before" category. Mel's method is definitely unique. The pointer finger on his right hand is bent and is the least controllable of his digits, so he uses a combination of his pointer and middle fingers. The contacts go right in on most days although it takes more time to take them out. Other days remain a struggle with sensation and dexterity limiting his efforts.

Donning Tefillin

Once upon a time, there was a secular Jewish girl who dated and then married an Orthodox Jewish boy. She was soon exposed to an inordinate number of new customs as the breadth of her understanding of Judaism increased exponentially. One thing she was peripherally aware of that occurred each weekday morning, and which she even viewed firsthand on the rare occasions that she attended morning services at a synagogue, was the practice of donning *tefillin*.

The English term for *tefillin* is phylacteries, a confusing and unenlightening term whose Greek origin means amulet. This holy ritual object is composed of two leather boxes that contain Biblical passages that are hand written on parchment. Leather straps are attached to each box, allowing the person praying to wrap one box around the forehead and the other around the non-dominant arm. Not being particularly egalitarian when it comes to Jewish ritual customs that are meant for men, the Jewish girl had no reason to learn the specifics of donning *tefillin*.

Fast-forward some 30 years and that Jewish girl now found herself in a less than ideal situation.

Mel was growing stronger every day due to his herculean efforts and exemplary faith. Almost instantaneously he transitioned from survival mode to being in the-world-of-the-living mode. And while his spirituality never left him, the ability to literally wrap himself in its outer physical trappings had to be put on hold.

Noting that putting on *tefillin*, a task which requires full dexterity in the fingers and hands, would be utterly impossible for Mel, our son-in-law Simcha offered to help Mel put them on for the first time post-accident. Mel's eyes lit up and he quickly agreed.

I rummaged through the shelving unit by Mel's bed and found his velvet covered *tefillin* bag pushed to the back of the top shelf. For almost a month the *tefillin* had been waiting for just this moment. Placing the bag on the tray table, I left Simcha and Mel and went outside in search of Becca and the girls.

When I returned to Mel's room, my eyes filled with tears at the beautiful sight of Mel and Simcha: blond and gray tinged heads bowed toward one another, two sets of sky blue eyes focused on the *tefillin* wrapped around Mel's arm, identical broad smiles on those handsome faces. It wasn't until that moment that I realized how difficult it must have been for Mel to miss performing this daily mitzvah for so long. It was one of those "Aha" moments when you realize how important something is to someone you love. Until now the thought hadn't crossed my mind. I suddenly realized that Mel had been missing and yearning for this tangible connection to his spiritual life.

"Actions that you do repeatedly become internalized, a part of your inner being," our rabbi said recently, in describing the meaning of performing *mitzvot*, or commandments. "This doesn't make them boring or uninteresting, rather, their repetition elevates you and gives you purpose."

Donning *tefillin* each day is one of those repetitive activities. I could literally see the meaning of our rabbi's words by looking at my two beaming men.

As the weekend came to a close, Simcha and Becca, along with our beautiful granddaughters, returned to New Jersey. This left a big void in our hearts as well as leaving us without our valiant Simcha to help Mel with his *tefillin*. It was now up to me to take his place.

There was only one problem.

I didn't have a clue about any of it. In fact, I had never even seen the process from start to finish, and I am pretty sure I am in the majority, along with most Jewish women who wouldn't know where to begin in performing this sacred ritual. The process is precise and requires hand dexterity. I began *tefillin*-wrapping lessons with Mel.

As with any Jewish ritual, there are mandatory rules and traditional customs which vary according to family tradition and countries of origin. The *tefillin* ritual falls into this category. While I was somewhat frustrated by the activity, I did stop to think about the beauty of fulfilling this commandment in the correct way. One little mistake and the *tefillin* won't sit correctly on the body. When done carefully, with mindfulness and precision, the *tefillin* ritual will be fulfilled in the way it was intended.

And so I followed Mel's directions in the proper order: removing the *tefillin* straps from the bag; first the arm box and then the head box. Next came the steps of how and where to place each piece on the body: The arm *tefillin* box inside the left arm, his non-dominant arm prior to the accident, on the bicep facing the heart. The strap is wrapped around the left arm seven times and then around the hand.

The *tefillin* for the head follows, the straps loop around the head with the box centered on the forehead between the eyes. The long leather straps are positioned to flow down the front of the body.

The ceremony ends with a series of steps involving the long strap being wound around the fingers and hand, again requiring agile fingers and hands.

All of this was done with minimal speaking and much head nodding.

After Mel finished his morning prayers, we would literally unravel the entire process in reverse order, carefully, slowly, and often with much frustration.

Each morning I went through all the required steps. Over the next number of weeks and months, as Mel gained dexterity in his hands and fingers, he began to take over as much as he could. Our little two-person dance that had me leading was slowly becoming a more equally shared *pas-de-deux*, and progressed to Mel taking on a more significant role. Eventually he was able to complete the entire process independently. Ecstatic to see Mel wrapping *tefillin* by himself, I happily relinquished my part but never lost my respect for this mitzvah which has been performed by Jewish men throughout the ages. Mel had fully rejoined the ranks.

As I write this, a few years have passed. Every now and then I attend morning services at the synagogue. With rapt fascination, I watch Mel don his *tefillin*, a silly smile spreading across my face. *Whatever is she thinking*, I imagine the women around me wonder when they notice my funny smile. *It's a long story*, I would tell them if they asked. *It ends with a little girl who learned how to put on tefillin but gladly gave it up.*

And they all lived happily ever after.

Return to Healing Garden

Two toddle and one runs across the little bridge overlooking the Healing Garden.

Our grandchildren squeal. Music.

The whole family together enjoying a short outing.

Our sons-in-law chasing after the kids, swooping up the two little ones, standing beside Mel. Their caring and protectiveness evident in the way each touches the back of the wheelchair as they speak to Mel about the kids, about the beautiful weather.

My gaze roams from face to precious face, landing on our daughters, talking softly to one another. They look at me and smile.

"What's up, Mom?" asks Becca.

Two daughters, each within a few short months of giving birth. My thoughts are focused on new life, new grandchildren. Questions begin to race through my mind.

When would we be able to meet the newest additions to our family? We certainly would not be there for the births this time, a disappointment for all of us. Would we logistically be able to visit? How would we travel? Would it be too difficult with wheelchairs and who knows what kinds of equipment? How often would we be able to see our children and grandchildren? Their visits would become more complicated as the families grew.

Shutting off the negativity, I remain hopeful even though the outlook seems bleak at this point. We'll make it happen, I insist to myself.

"Just so glad everyone's here together," I sing out, sitting beside Yael on a bench shaded by a small tree.

Shira skids to a halt in front of Mel. In his big electric wheelchair, with his gaping smile and huge neck brace, I worry that three year old Shira may be a bit hesitant and frightened. Not our Shira. She looks at Mel with such love and adoration that my heart overflows.

"Hi, Shira Beara, do you want to come up and sit on my lap?" Mel asks.

She nods her head with a big smile.

Becca lifts her up, and she turns her body to face Mel. She cuddles close to him.

"I love you Saba."

"I love you too, Shira."

The picture is in my mind's eye forever.

Jack appears a short while later.

"I found all of you," he says, patting Mel's back.

"Hi, Jack. How did you figure out where we were?" I ask.

"One of Mel's nurses thought you headed this way," he replies.

With hellos all around, Jack zeroes in on the children. Jack loves kids and they adore him. Immediately, he gravitates to Eliora and Akiva. Squatting, he makes silly faces and goofy sounds. Shira scrambles off from Mel's lap and joins the action. Giggles from all three are testimony to his success in entertaining them.

Way before I was ready — which would have been never if anyone asked — it is time for the group to go. Jack leaves first, giving us privacy. The kids need naps, Becca and Simcha need to drive back home to New Jersey and Yael has classes back at college. Shana and Moshe are scheduled to return to Israel the next day and need to go back to our house to pack. Moshe pushes Mel's chair as we all slowly walk to the front door of the building. I don't know where we find the strength, but we manage our goodbyes.

Mel and I remain outside and watch the group move away. "We'll see them soon. Don't worry," he says.

We both fall silent.

"It will be okay," he says as I wheel him back to his room.

To see our faces, one wouldn't have been so sure.

Day 23

May 26, 2013

Sunday is the day of rest here in the world of Kernan. Without the structure of the therapy workweek, Mel was able to slow the pace and enjoy some time with our children and grandchildren outside in the gardens. With the help of our son Simcha, Mel was able, for the first time since the accident, to put on tefillin and daven some of the morning tefillot. What a beautiful sight! Please continue to pray with Mel for a full recovery and excellent outcome.

Happy Birthday Mel!

"Can I bring a few of the Ravens to visit Mel for his birthday?" Dave asked as he, Gary and I stood in the hallway outside Mel's door at the end of his first week at Kernan. Mel's 'birthday twin' wanted to do something special for his friend. A real people person, Dave seems to know everyone and have connections worldwide.

"I don't know. I'm not sure he'll be up for it."

"Don't worry Judy, he'll love it," he pressed.

"He'll love it," Gary agreed.

Tacitly, the decision was finalized. Dave organized the impromptu birthday party to bring three of the Baltimore Ravens to Mel's hospital room. The party grew as a few of our friends joined us in the late afternoon.

The room was abuzz. Ravens players in purple and black football jerseys surrounded Mel in his wheelchair. They spoke to him about injury and recovery.

"It's one of the hardest things you'll ever do, but you'll be stronger for it," one of the football players said. The others nodded in agreement. Mel looked up into their faces as they told him they would pray for his recovery, a huge grin splitting his face.

As the noise and excitement level increased, I worried that the Kernan nurses would come to reprimand us. Instead, they were all smiles as they peeked their heads in the doorway, their birthday wishes mingling with those of the group.

Day 25

May 28, 2013

I held our grandson as we watched two of Mel's birthday balloons escape into the sky. As I remember his adorable fascination with the rapidly ascending balloons, it makes me think of how quickly Mel has progressed. May Hashem make Mel's difficulties vanish quickly and leave clear skies in their wake.

Mel's trach procedure was successful and he now has a smaller tube. The Ear-Nose-Throat doctor was very encouraging. He believes that the trach will be removed in the next few weeks. Each thing that is removed is a huge step forward! Tomorrow is the swallow test. Please daven extra hard for Mel's success.

Thank you to all who shared in Mel's birthday wishes and all the special things that were done to cheer him on this day.

Speech Therapy at Kernan

Another speech therapist entered our lives once Mel moved to Kernan. Tricia's job was to help Mel with his tracheostomy and speech through the valve, as well as continuing testing and preparing him for his next swallow test. Tricia's caring demeanor made this roller coaster ride of recovery activities a bit more palatable.

The process for tracheostomy removal is a stepwise progression. Tricia led us to an office on the other side of the building for Mel's appointment with the ENT specialist. The doctor replaced his tracheostomy tube with a slightly smaller one. This happened twice during a two-week period. At the third appointment the doctor approved the removal of Mel's tracheostomy. At our request, Dr. Y., Mel's physiatrist, performed the actual removal late on the second Friday afternoon at Kernan. A small bandage was placed over the hole in Mel's throat.

"It will close up in a week or so," Dr. Y. explained. "Then we'll remove the bandage. The scar will be very small and not so noticeable. Mel, you have done remarkably well."

A small scar remains in the middle of Mel's throat, a reminder of how we should not take anything for granted, even the most basic life function: breathing.

***

The road to a successful swallow test took a bit longer. The failure of the first attempt increased our anxiety. Tricia practiced with Mel, giving him tiny amounts of different fluids to drink very slowly. Mel would cough and sputter, signaling that the fluid was flowing down the wrong tube.

Repeated failures were extremely dangerous as aspiration was life threatening. Yet the practice continued. Around a week or so later, Tricia felt Mel was ready to try the test again.

Mel, Tricia and I were all subdued as she led us once again to the office on the far side of the building. The same doctor and assistant greeted us. I assumed my position in the small hallway, fervent prayers flowing from my lips. "Please let me make the dash to 7-Eleven today."

In just a few short minutes the door opened. The mood was not as somber as the last time. "Mel passed part of the test," Tricia said. "He's able to manage thicker liquids."

"That's good, right?" I asked.

"Yes. It is good, but a bit unusual. He wasn't able to properly drink the thinner fluids, only the thicker ones."

"What does that mean for him? Should I go get a Slurpee?"

"Yes. Go get a Slurpee!" she exclaimed. "He deserves it."

"What flavor should I get, Mel?" I asked.

"You know what? I think I want a Rita's ice instead."

"Great! What flavor?"

"Cherry or Cotton Candy," was his quick response.

"I'm on it," I said. "Tricia, will you get him back to his room while I run?"

"Sure," she said laughing. In fact, everyone in the room was laughing.

Day 26

May 29, 2013

I wish you all had been here to see the look of joy on Mel's face as he recited the bracha and swallowed his first taste of cotton candy flavored Rita's ice! The swallow test yielded some success and Mel can now enjoy liquids including ices, ice cream, and smooth soups. Some of the best foods known to man! When the time came, Mel chose the ice over the slurpee, but I think a big slurpee is on tap for tomorrow and many days to come.

On a breathing note, the trach is now smaller and today they began to plug the trach instead of using a speaking valve. This allows Mel to breathe in and out through his nose or mouth in essence as we all do, He is flying through this new advancement and I think the trach days are almost over.

Therapy is also going very well. As Beth, Mel's PT said today, "Each day I see new muscles working."

It really is miraculous to behold and we thank Hashem throughout each day. Please continue to daven for continued daily improvement. As many of the healthcare workers have said, "This is a marathon not a sprint."

Transfers – A Necessity

While at Shock Trauma, it was vital for Mel to spend at least an hour each day, preferably two, in a chair in order to prevent pressure sores. The method of transfer from the bed to the chair was something I was not privy to during Mel's time at Shock Trauma. The staff would ask me to kindly step outside until Mel was situated. So it was not until the first day at Kernan that I had my initial glimpse into the difficult process.

A special apparatus is often used to transfer paralyzed patients from bed to chair or wheelchair. The ones at Kernan were mechanical Hoyer Lifts. I thought that the apparatus was called a Hoyer Lift, and it wasn't until much later that I realized Hoyer was the brand name of the device. The lift includes a metal base on rollers with an adjustable arm that moves vertically and is connected to a horizontal free-moving bar with multiple hooks to attach the sling. The sling is made of heavy material and is very similar to a hammock. The sling is placed under the patient and is then attached by its corner grommets to the hooks on the horizontal crossbar.

Slowly and carefully, the lift's arm is raised sometimes mechanically, sometimes manually, and the patient is raised off the bed. Extreme care must be taken to prevent the arm and horizontal bar from swinging too freely as the lift is moved toward a waiting chair. The patient is positioned above the chair and the arm is lowered slowly. With precision and luck, the patient will then be sitting in the chair bundled in the sling. The sling is unhooked from the crossbar and removed by rolling the patient to one side and pulling out the released portion of the sling. The patient is rolled to the other side and again the released portion is pulled away until the patient is sitting sling free. The process is cumbersome and takes a significant amount of time, but it is a huge physical help to the caregiver, whose only other option is to bodily lift the patient.

In those early weeks, I watched morning and evening as Mel was transferred with the Hoyer lifts. It is an incredibly humbling experience to be exposed to this display of complete and utter dependence. I know it shook me to the core as I watched my proud husband being relocated in the apparatus. The emotional toll must have been significant for Mel, although he rarely complained. The need to get into the wheelchair so that he could get to therapy was the driving force, the rock to which he clung.

Four weeks went by. The genius behind Mel's clever and talented therapists became evident. They started talking about transfers. Bit by bit, muscle by muscle, they began working on functionality. From the first painstaking moments sitting hunched over the side of the therapy table nearly falling off with zero core strength, to the first baby push against the floor with his feet, to the first assisted triceps exercise, they had been rebuilding Mel. All the elements needed to come together in order to achieve the monumental task of transferring his weight from bed to chair and chair to bed, and I watched in awe as it began to happen.

At first, Mel was able to help the aides in small but significant ways. Moving his feet to the side of the bed was a big accomplishment. In the early stages, a flat wooden transfer board about two feet long and eight inches wide was wedged under his bottom, connecting the space between bed and chair. The nurses or aides would stand in front of Mel, bend their knees, grasp him under his armpits and lift him along the transfer board to his seat. Mel would help as much as he could to plant his feet on the ground and push down on the board and far side of the chair's arm with his arms and hands. To see his progress day by day was to see a world of possibilities open up: showering with a bath seat, getting into a car, a bus, a plane. Functionality – not a given but a blessing – was something to be grasped and appreciated.

His progress gained momentum, and shortly before his release from inpatient therapy, Mel could transfer almost independently. When I took him for his first home visit two weeks prior to release, Mel transferred seamlessly into the car using the transfer board without any human assistance. With beaming faces, Beth, his extraordinary PT, and I cheered.

Often during the first few months, people asked me if Mel was going to walk again. I tried not to be impatient with their innocent yet ignorant questions. Walking? Who could imagine walking? It felt like a distant dream, an almost unimaginable goal. We had so many serious issues to deal with that eclipsed the dream.

"I believe he will," I would answer, "but he needs to be able to transfer first." Transfers were a hopeful possibility, a daily prayer.

Mel had perfected transfers by the time he went home, just shy of the three-month mark after the accident. Our prayers had been answered not only in the affirmative, but in the resounding affirmative. Through sweat, tears, and the amazing dedication of his superb therapists, Mel had gained the necessary strength to transfer without the board. Beth gave him a transfer board to take home just in case. It sits unopened in its original wrapping in the corner of our basement.

Tenodesis

As an inpatient at Kernan, Mel had his daily Occupational Therapy session promptly at 9:30 each morning. The session's activities progressed as Mel progressed, but each session began with assisted stretching of his hands and fingers. Lauren taught me how to hold Mel's hands and arms, how and where to apply pressure, and the order of the series of stretches. The goal of the assisted stretches was to preserve as much range of motion in his muscles and joints as possible, so the functionality would be there if and when Mel advanced to a point where he was ready and able to use them. Severe tone, the contraction of the muscles in response to the lack of motion and muscle memory, is a serious problem with spinal cord injuries. Passive stretching is essential when the injured person is unable to actively participate. Some tone can be worked through and lessened over time with a great deal of effort and focused practice, but some tone unfortunately cannot be overcome. Even though he made incredible progress, spasticity, the uncontrolled tightening of the muscles, continues to be a challenge for Mel.

During the first few weeks of recovery, there was a true need and desire to retain the tone, specifically the contraction of Mel's finger muscles. This was done to provide the very real and necessary need to hold utensils. For the knowledge of anatomy-challenged (of which I am surely a member), the theory is this: There is a synergistic, anatomical connection between flexing the wrist, the wrist seemingly flopping forward like a puppy dog paw, and the extensors of the fingers. As the wrist bends away from the arm, the hand relaxes down and extends. The opposite is true as well. As the wrist extends, much like the Queen of England's famous wave, the fingers and hand move closer to the arm and the fingers contract, bending and closing up a bit. This anatomical connection is called tenodesis[6], and can be the difference between complete dependence and an impressive amount of autonomy.

With virtual fingers crossed, I watched as Lauren taught Mel how to flex his wrist and use the associated extension of the fingers to grasp a plastic spoon. This was no small feat. Mel had not held anything in his fingers, even a weightless tissue, for over four weeks. There had been attempts and even some success in communication while at Shock Trauma using a pencil strapped to his wrist brace, but that was a far cry from the finesse of manipulating something with his atrophied fingers.

I watched as Mel made many attempts at grasping the spoon, his fingers brushing the white spoon around on the tabletop, repeatedly gaining and losing partial grasp. With a half-smile on his face, he finally gained some semblance of control over the spoon.

Grasping is one thing. Holding is another.

Lauren taught Mel how to raise his arm, extend his wrist, and after much practice, triumphantly hold the spoon aloft in

---

[6] Tenodesis grasp and release is an orthopedic observation of a passive hand grasp and release mechanism, effected by wrist extension or flexion, respectively. It is caused by the manner of attachment of the finger tendons to the bones and the passive tension created by two-joint muscles used to produce a functional movement or task (tenodesis).

Jeff G. Konin, (1999) Slack, Inc., Practical Kinesiology for the Physical Therapist Assistant, p. 19.

https://en.wikipedia.org/wiki/Tenodesis_grasp

his closed, contracted fingers. After much grunting, the spoon had been conquered. I let out a big exhale and smiled. Mel was exhausted but happy.

One for Mel, fifty-three for the spoon.

Male Grooming

A few weeks into Mel's stay at Kernan, he complained that his scalp was itchy. His triceps were still very weak and he couldn't raise his hands to his head. His fingers could not do an adequate job of scratching with the amount of tone he had and the lack of finger dexterity and strength. "Do the nurses wash your hair when they wash you in the mornings?" I asked.

"They wouldn't spend any time doing that," he said. His negative response startled me. I realized that yet another activity of daily living had been neglected. Washing Mel's hair was a challenge. The huge neck collar Mel continued to wear for twelve full weeks in order to immobilize his neck and keep it safe while healing from the surgeries was quite the obstacle. It would be uncomfortable if it got wet, and I didn't want Mel to get a rash or sore. Appealing to the nursing staff for a solution, I was handed a bag filled with microwaveable dry shampoo. I wondered why they had not been using it to wash his hair prior to my asking.

As Mel tilted back into a pressure release, I went to the common area in the unit and used the microwave to warm the mixture. I slowly massaged the warm shampoo into Mel's hair making sure to stay clear of the neck brace. A smile lit up his face. "That feels amazing," he said. I could only imagine. It had been at least a month since his head and scalp had been marginally clean.

While we were in grooming mode, I brought out the electric shaver and cleaned his growing stubble. I found shaving Mel to be a big chore. His beard was very thick and I didn't want to press the shaver too hard, worried that the pressure would affect his neck. It took a long time to make a decent impact. As his fingers and hands gained dexterity and strength, Mel thankfully took on more and more of this arduous task.

Eventually, he needed a haircut. After being married for over 25 years, I was surprised to realize that I had no idea what Mel's hair was supposed to look like. With a brand new hair clipper in hand, I hovered behind him, hesitant to begin. Our friends David and Liz had come to visit. David tried to direct me but I was clueless. "I'll do it," David offered, laughing. Gratefully, I gave over the task to him, glad to relinquish control. Male grooming was a full-time job.

At the end of the marathon length days, when things got a big quieter, I often planned to wash his hair or give him a shave. More often than not, I would have to postpone the plan either because of late visitors or sheer exhaustion.

"Can it wait another day?" I would ask Mel.

"Of course," he would always reply, although I knew he was disappointed.

Thoughtful Food

Keeping kosher is rather easy to do living in Baltimore, Maryland. We have dairy and meat restaurants, most of the local markets have kosher sections and a wide selection of products, and we even have two full service kosher supermarkets with meat, fish and prepared foods departments. Some of the hospitals offer kosher food as an option.

On the day of the accident when our thoughts were far from food, many caring individuals realized what we needed and jumped into action. Calls were made, food was ordered, and a stocked mini-fridge was brought to the hospital. *Bikur Cholim*, a charitable organization in our community, provided everything. It wasn't until much later that I truly understood the magnitude of the giving and the commitment of the caring volunteers involved with this beautiful organization.

On day three, I received a call on my cell. Pam and Sherri forced me away from Mel's bedside to head outside for a few minutes. Enjoying the warmth of sun and friendship, the three of us sat on a bench under a big elm tree in the small urban park across the street from the University of Maryland Medical Center.

"I don't know who this is," I said looking at the phone number. I answered anyway, and a pleasant female voice responded.

"Hi, Mrs. Pachino, this is Malki. I volunteer with *Bikur Cholim*."

"Oh Malki, thank you so much for the food and the refrigerator. I don't know what we would've done without them over the weekend," I gushed.

"I'm so glad it helped. Was the food all right? Did you have enough?"

"More than enough. There were only two of us but enough food for at least ten. We have plenty of delicious leftovers for the next few days."

"That's great. Also, that's why I'm calling. I've been assigned as your coordinator. My job is to connect with you and organize meals for however long you need them."

Pointing to the phone, I looked at Pam and Sherri. "*Bikur Cholim*," I whispered. "That would be amazing. I can't tell you how much I appreciate your help right now."

"Wonderful. I work at the hospital, so we can meet to go over what you might need over the next few days. How about if I stop in to see you tomorrow?"

"That would be perfect."

"Can I send you fresh food for today?"

"Oh I don't think that's necessary. I have plenty left over."

Malki asked again if I wanted anything more sent that day and then hung up. She would become a true friend over the next few months. Always there with a smile that I could see in person and hear on the phone, she took incredible care of us. A more beautiful soul one would be hard-pressed to find. She probably sent us more than a hundred meals, feeding Mel and me, and our family, too, when they came to visit. This was all done through the largesse of this amazing charity.

For Shabbat, our friends Sherri, Pam and Malka stepped in, organizing homemade meals prepared with love by a wide range of our friends. Love was the operative word, and we felt it in the care and attention to the packaging, in the abundance of food and in its heartwarming tastes.

At Shock Trauma, I had an additional food resource of a stocked refrigerator in a small conference room on the other side of the hospital. Malki showed me the way one afternoon in our first week there. As she entered a code into the keypad on the locked cabinet in the rear of the room, she explained that a volunteer stocked the refrigerator weekly and removed out-of-date or spoiled foods and refilled staples as well as treats. This food was there for anyone who needed. "Please take anything you want," she said. Throughout our ordeal, I was inspired by the realization that there is such good in the world. It had a huge impact on me.

Once Mel was at Kernan and had passed his swallow test, he started to get a tray of food at mealtimes. Kernan did not have a kosher option, but unbelievably the hospital sent one of its food service staff to Seven Mile Market, the kosher market in Pikesville, to pick up prepared foods for Mel. We were amazed at this extraordinary development. It was a good half-hour drive from the hospital to the store. Although the staff was incredibly receptive, especially the two young men who were charged with Mel's special needs, we were careful not to overwhelm them, only asking for lunch items that could last a few days. Many of the breakfast items used at the hospital were also permissible. Mel did not go hungry.

Our undying gratitude goes out to each and every person who made sure the refrigerators were well-stocked and our hearts and bodies lovingly fed.

Recreational Therapy

One especially bright and shining presence at Kernan was Mike, the recreational therapist. Injured in an accident when he was in his teens, Mike zips around the hospital in his wheelchair wearing a big welcoming smile on his youthful face.

It was Mel's third week at Kernan, just after his morning OT session, when Mike appeared at Mel's door.

"Time for recreational therapy," he called out. "Follow me please."

Perplexed, Mel and I followed. No one had mentioned recreational therapy, whatever that might be.

Mike led us past the gym, down the hallway and around a corner to his office. The room was crowded with Mike's desk, a large activity table in the middle of the room, a few chairs around the table, a bookshelf stuffed with books and games and Mike's and Mel's wheelchairs. I took a seat in one of the folding chairs and listened as Mike described his role at Kernan. We quickly learned that Mike uses assorted games and sports-like activities and a variety of tricks and tools as well as loads of enthusiasm to motivate and further a patient's functionality.

Mel was scheduled to meet with Mike once a week. I could see the skepticism and sadness on his face as he looked at his hands and fingers. I could guess his thoughts. How in the world will I do anything with these hands? They barely move. They are useless. What game could I play?

Mel is a sports guy; he loves to play, to watch, and to teach sports, especially basketball and tennis. Again I thought that perhaps things were moving too quickly. It seemed premature, and I worried that Mel would be overwhelmed, or worse, disillusioned.

Mike was undaunted. He told Mel that he would pick him up the next day at noon to play ping-pong.

"Be ready," he said. "You're gonna love it."

I held my tongue, and was glad I did when Mel returned the next day after playing with Mike.

"Mike wrapped my hands around the paddles with surgical tape, so I could move my arms and swing," he said excitedly. "I tried both arms and I played pretty well. At first I missed a lot, but then I got the hang of it, and I made a few good shots!"

The moment wasn't lost on me. It was the first time Mel had expressed pure excitement since the accident. Sports. I should have guessed. The short half-hour session with Mike had opened him up. He was more alive; he saw possibilities. It's not that Mel wasn't motivated or positive until now. But this was different. Here was something that helped him connect with the old Mel, the pre-accident guy, the sports fanatic. The joy on his face said it all. He recovered a bit of himself amidst his injured shell.

Mel continued to meet with Mike weekly. They often played ping-pong, Mike wrapping Mel's hands less and less as they became more functional. Eventually, Mel's hands were strong enough to hold the paddles; the roll of surgical tape lay untouched on the table. Mel always came back filled with excitement, recounting the better points and making sure I knew who won. Often it was Mel.

One afternoon, Mel returned from his session with Mike and told me that he and Mike had been riding around the parking lot on recumbent bikes. Shocked at first, I listened as he explained his initial nervousness and hesitation then his

142

actual enjoyment of the activity. The thought of Mel riding on a bike surrounded by cars was not a warm, fuzzy one for me, but I tried to be supportive nonetheless. Mel was excited, so I should be excited.

Throughout the week, Mike led group activity sessions. Mel enjoyed the camaraderie and challenge so we often joined in. A few of the games we played included Flag Toss on the grassy area in front of the building, and Bowling in the Halls, a challenging and fun game for the participants. I helped Mike set up the pins and retrieve the balls while the patients lined up and competed. The cheering and laughter from the group filled the hallway with beautiful positive energy and hope.

Mike was more than someone who played games with the patients at Kernan. He inspired them, made them smile and truly brightened their days. I know that he was thinking about taking a new job near the end of Mel's time at Kernan, but I never found out if he decided to leave.

I hope that wherever he ended up, Mike knows what a difference he made in Mel's life. He made the "other therapy" a highlight of Mel's nearly ten weeks at Kernan.

Day 31

June 3, 2013

Mel had his regular OT and PT therapy today, but he also enjoyed a new type of therapy for him, recreational therapy. We were both a bit skeptical when Mike pulled us in for an impromptu half hour, but Mel was quickly engaged in a game of gin rummy with REGULAR cards. I watched as Mel used fine motor skills that I didn't think possible at this early stage. Amazing!!! P.S. Mel won.

Day 32

June 4, 2013

Today was another day moving forward. Mel's trach size was reduced to the smallest one (four millimeters), and he is now set for the plug trial. The trach will be plugged with a little plastic insert day and night for two days. If all goes well, the trach may be removed this Friday and the breathing issues completely resolved! It was truly a relief when the ENT doctor announced today that Mel's airway was beautifully clear and dry. The surgeries have not created any problems in his airway and we are sincerely grateful. Mel told his sister by phone today that he sees and feels the yad Hashem in each movement as he progresses. I think that is awesome!

Day 33

June 5, 2013

The start of week three at Kernan went well. OT and PT were challenging. One day down with the trach plug trial and cruising along. Mel is working on his swallowing and preparing for more solid type foods hopefully in the near future. The wonders never cease.

For the first time today, Mel was able to hold a juice carton and drink it with complete independence. I was privileged to witness this beautiful achievement! Please continue to pray and learn on Mel's behalf. Hashem is most certainly listening and responding!

Day 34

June 6, 2013

Mel returned from a forty-minute ping pong match with Mike (rec therapy) a huge grin lighting his adorable face. Exhausted but happy, he recounted the use of both hands and his angling skill. No rest time though here at Kernan. Next up was speech therapy and practice swallowing for tomorrow's big swallow test. A questionable practice lunch of pudding, fruit cup and matzah balls was handled with aplomb and then he was off to his afternoon of OT and PT. Mel didn't let a rampant rash slow him down one bit even though it took some time to get relief. What an inspiration he is each and every day!

The Rash

"Guess what?" Mel asked me as soon as I arrived in the morning.

"What?"

"Do you notice anything missing from my nose?"

"I don't think so."

"The feeding tube."

"What happened to it? Did the doctor take it out so early?"

"Not exactly."

"Well….?" I prompted.

"The aides were rough this morning. They flung me around more than usual and my tube got caught on something. Yanked it right out."

"Was it painful?"

"Only when they tried to force it back in. Then I told them to just leave it out, because it was scheduled to be removed this afternoon."

"What did they say?"

"Okay."

"No apology?"

"Nope."

Day 36

June 9, 2013

Friday was a record day! Mel's feeding tube came out and the trach was removed in the afternoon. He looks great without the tubes and metal! We entered Shabbat with relief that the big medical issues are resolved. He is now able to eat most foods and it is a joy for him! Eating is another gift that we often take for granted.

The weather cooperated and we were able to spend some time outside on Shabbat lifting our spirits and instilling the day with some beauty.

I would like to once again (although this is a constant) thank the truly awesome volunteers for bringing and the organization of Bikur Cholim for providing food daily. It has been five long weeks, and I am touched and fed each day by their continual chesed.

Thank you also to Jewish Caring Network for the gift basket this Shabbat. Amazing!

Please know that we hear from each of you by the Caring Bridge, by phone, by cards, by messages, by texts and we are blessed to have so many people rooting and showing such genuine concern for us. Mel's days are very, very busy and this is grueling work. We would love to open the door for all to come and visit, but he would simply be overwhelmed and not get the rest that he needs. We thank you for understanding.

It was Friday again and Shabbat was looming ahead. Facing another Shabbat at Kernan was something neither Mel nor I were looking forward to. Instead, it was a trial of faith, one that we could never have imagined.

This time, Sherri had organized and gathered an assortment of delicious foods packed into small, manageable plastic containers, her trademark efficient organizational skills in action. She included pretty plates and fancy cutlery in a gesture of love and an attempt to elevate our meals to more than what they were – sad, lonely affairs, eaten in a communal setting where the television droned on, the staff entered and exited with marked comments about our meal, other patients and their families visiting, and the dinner cleanup – scraping and rinsing of dishes by the staff. Someone's family dog came to visit and it accompanied us during our meal, sniffing us and especially our food.

After I heated the food in the microwave using two layers of plastic wrap for kosher reasons, I set the table, and Mel rolled in. I left him with the food and returned to Mel's room to turn on the electric candelabra and usher in the Shabbat. As I did, I reflected on the fact that another Shabbat had passed without lighting real candles, yet another week had passed that would bring us closer to normal life. I turned and strode out of the door, carrying Kiddush cup number three.

The food was very good. Our attempt at bringing a bit of holiness into the mundane with our quiet Kiddush was met with puzzled looks. Welcome to Shabbat, Week Number Five. Mel carried the drinks and managed his electric chair as I juggled the leftover food stacked in a 9x13 foil pan. We returned to Mel's room. It was 9 p.m., I noted, as I slid the last leftovers back into the refrigerator.

I looked over at Mel and noticed he was trying to scratch his neck without success.

"What's the matter?" I asked moving in for a look.

"Do you see anything on my neck?" he asked.

"Yes, you have some red spots on your neck," I replied with concern. By the time I had gotten the words out, I saw him start to rub at his right arm where red dots were forming.

"Do you see something on my arm?"

"Yeah," I said lifting his shirt and venturing a look at his chest. "I think you have a rash again," I replied, keeping my voice as even as possible. He had an irritating rash earlier in the week that had seemed to go away.

Red welts were appearing before my eyes. They were forming all over his body in rapid succession.

"I'm going to get the nurse."

I hurried down the hall and found our nurse, Lawrence, about to enter another patient's room.

"Mel has a rash and its spreading by the second. Please come now, he needs help. We have to get ahead of it!" I started back to Mel's room, compelling him to follow.

Lawrence did follow and quickly looked Mel over. Sure enough, the rash was in force, covering much of Mel's body. In the few short minutes it took to get help, the rash had sprung up all over his torso and legs, from neck to toes.

"I'll contact the doctor on call," Lawrence said calmly.

We knew this was not going to be fun. It was the weekend and we knew it was not a time to need anything but the basics.

"Are the doctors on site?" I asked.

Yes. We have someone in the hospital."

"Someone?" I asked with growing concern. "Do you mean that there is only one doctor for the whole hospital?"

"Yes. On the weekends, there is just one doctor on call."

"Oh," I said shaking my head in disbelief.

"I'll call the doctor," Lawrence said. He turned and left the room. Mel had remained silent throughout the exchange.

"Can you scratch my arm?" he asked looking at me. The misery in his eyes reflected the defeat we both felt. How much more could one person take? I thought.

"Of course," I replied pulling up a chair beside him and settling in to scratch.

About an hour had come and gone and no doctor had appeared. I went out to the hallway in search of Lawrence.

"Mel's miserable; where's the doctor?" I asked when I saw him coming out of the supply closet at the end of the hall.

"I did call. I'll call again," he answered.

"Mel's so uncomfortable. We really need to get him some help quickly. Please, is there anything we can do to get the doctor to come?" I pleaded.

"Let me see if we can give him some medicine to take the edge off. I'll ask the doctor."

"Okay," I responded unhappily, although that was not the answer I was looking for. "Please, do what you can."

I returned to Mel's bedside. The night technician had already helped him into bed while I was out. Bright red welts covered his entire body – even the spaces between his fingers and toes. Panic set in as I looked him over. I needed to get him help now!

Lawrence came in again and immediately saw just how bad the rash was. Within minutes, he brought an Atarax tablet and a cup of water. He helped Mel take the pill, supporting his back and head in a more upright position. Mel seemed all right with this temporary solution, and he explained to me that Atarax is an antihistamine used to combat symptoms of an allergic reaction, most specifically itching.

"The doctor is handling some admissions now, but he said he'll be over to check you when he's finished," Lawrence said to Mel.

"Is there any way to convince him to come sooner?" I asked.

"Mrs. Pachino, I will make sure the doctor comes. I'll keep calling. I'll do whatever I can," he answered, looking me in the eye.

"Thank you," I replied in earnest.

150

I sat by Mel's bedside and scratched his arms and hands. He lay quietly, completely focused on surviving the next moment. Thankfully, the Atarax, along with his nightly Ambien, took the edge off, and Mel fell asleep. I moved to the cot beside his bed and tried to calm myself down. It was just short of 11 p.m. and I was feeling the full weight of the world on my shoulders. I was Mel's advocate, the only one who could see to it that he got what he needed.

I started my vigil.

For the next two hours I waited. Every half-hour, I pulled my exhausted self off the cot and went to the nurses' station to ask about the doctor. Each time the nurse told me he was coming. At 1 a.m. I hit my limit. I marched to the nurses' station to ask about the doctor once again.

"He's busy with other patients," the head nurse said.

I looked her in the eye and broke my own rule of politeness.

"I know you don't care," I said with conviction. "My husband is miserable. He needs help, before the rash is completely out of control. I know you don't care at all," I muttered turning away. I was so tired that no tears would come to my eyes, but my heart was breaking.

I crawled back under the covers on the cot and listened to the sound of Mel's breathing. That alone brought me some hope, since breathing had been such a critical concern just a few shorts weeks ago.

At 1:20 a.m., the doctor entered the room followed by the vigilant Lawrence. He turned on the overhead lights and Mel groggily woke up and answered the doctor's questions. They discussed medications and decided it was best to start a Medrol Dosepak even though the origin of the rash was a mystery. The doctor assured us that he would put the order into the computer immediately and left with our thanks.

"I'll watch for the medicine and bring it to you as soon as possible," Lawrence added as he followed the doctor out. Within half an hour, Lawrence, good to his word, helped Mel take the first dose.

"Thank you so much for sticking with us on this, Lawrence," Mel said as he sank back into the pillows.

I watched the exchange, added my own sentiments of gratitude and then gratefully laid down to rest. Please God, I added silently, please let the medicine work quickly, for tomorrow is coming fast. The nurses will be in to wake him in no time.

I guess Lawrence filled the staff in on what happened, because they let us sleep until seven the next morning. When Mel woke up, the rash was somewhat under control; the red color was more pinkish, and the itching had lessened considerably.

Shabbat was unbearably long once again, yet I felt at ease. A crisis had been handled. Mel was relatively comfortable and able to work through his therapy. He even managed to rest a bit. That made it all good.

Mel continued the treatment throughout the weekend. The rash remained manageable but didn't seem to be getting significantly better. Looking for help, I mentioned the rash on my CaringBridge blog Sunday morning, specifically asking readers to pray for Mel's relief from the nasty rash. A response quickly came from a caring dermatologist in our community.

I received an email message that had been converted from voice to text by our phone company. Often the messages are scrambled and difficult to understand from the voice to text system, but this one was remarkably clear.

"Mel, Dr. K. called. He said he would be willing to come to the hospital to look at your rash if you want," I paraphrased.

"Sure. Tell him to come," Mel replied without hesitation.

"Okay. I'm on it," I responded, grateful for something constructive to do.

I immediately pulled out my cell phone and dialed the number on the message. The doctor's wife answered. Once I identified myself, she immediately asked how Mel was doing. She said that both she and her husband follow his progress daily on the blog. I mentioned her husband's phone message and asked to speak with him. He wasn't at home. Quickly locating pen and paper, she began to jot down my number. During this exchange, her husband returned and she put me on hold while she brought him up to speed about Mel.

"How's Mel doing?" he asked.

"To be honest," I replied, "the rash is really a concern. It doesn't seem to be improving. Are you still able to come by and take a look?"

"Of course. In fact, I'll come right now if that's good for Mel."

"Right now? That would be amazing! Thank you so much."

"What's the room number?"

"It's 821. Keep right after the main reception desk, then left at the turn, straight to the end and then left."

"Tell Mel I'm on my way."

Excitedly, I relayed the message to Mel.

Thirty minutes later, Dr. K. walked through the door to Mel's hospital room. In just two minutes the kind doctor completed his exam, determined a diagnosis and recommended a course of action.

The exam consisted of one minute glancing at the different exposed areas of Mel's body, followed by two questions.

"Did you have any infections while at Shock Trauma?" the good doctor asked.

"Yes, a urinary tract infection."

"What did they give you for the UTI?"

"Levaquin," Mel and I answered together.

"Well that's your answer. Initial allergic reactions to Levaquin and the quinolone class of antibiotics take up to two weeks to emerge," Dr. K. said.

It had been exactly two weeks to the day when the first rash appeared. Instead of controlling the reaction, Medrol, which was simply not powerful enough, had only lessened the effects. A much stronger course of steroids was needed. Dr. K. discussed this with Dr. Y. the next day, and a high dosage of Prednisone was prescribed. Within a few days, the rash crisis was history.

They say it takes a village. I agree. I think it takes an amazing community filled with caring people who are willing to reach out and help, sharing their unique talents for the good of others. Dr. K. answered the call to help and saved Mel countless hours of discomfort at a time when every ounce of energy he could muster was needed for recovery from his injury rather than fighting off medicinal side effects.

I started the blog at Nurse Karen's urging. She had insisted people would want to follow Mel's progress, to know what was happening. It will be a great way to share information, she told me.

Many were reading my posts from the CaringBridge website, but I later learned that a friend from the community, someone Mel grew up with, ran his own website, *Baltimore Jewish Life*. Every day, Jeff copied and posted my blog entry into an ongoing column titled, "Because We All Love Mel," sending my words deeper into cyberspace and reaching countless more caring hearts. Never would I have guessed the blog's impact on a community and individual level.

After we were home from the hospital, it was a common occurrence for people from our beautiful community to stop me on the street or in a store and tell me how much they appreciated my entries. They touched me with their sincere desire to be of help and to know and be there for Mel. To a person, I was told that they found perspective through Mel's recovery. His example of grit and determination helped them find the strength to deal with their own challenges. The outpouring of caring and love was palpable.

The rash was just one example of the power of the blog. Mel needed help. I sent the message out. Help appeared instantaneously in the form of a caring doctor from our community.

Night Terrors

When darkness falls, our vulnerabilities emerge and our insecurities intensify. We feel exposed and unsure. So we scurry home in search of safety and protection and surround ourselves with things that comfort us. We may leave lights on throughout the house or keep televisions droning to stave off the feelings that night evokes. But in a hospital, even with lights glaring and televisions blaring, keeping those monsters at bay takes superhuman resolve.

Mel was terrified of the nights. The nighttime routine of undressing and getting situated for the long hours ahead was both physically and emotionally brutal. Exhausted from the day's efforts, he tried to hold out at long as possible before pressing the call button to set the evening's routine in motion. Eventually he was forced into action. I would usually stay to make sure he was settled, picking out the next day's clothes and running the selection by him. Sometimes he would have a preference, but mostly his interest was barely piqued.

Mel's night nurse would arrive in answer to the call request, bringing the evening medications. Then the aide was told that Mel was ready.

Could he really be ready for the nightly horror of his bedtime routine?

What does it mean to have a spinal cord injury? What does it mean to have one's muscles atrophy to nothing, to have one's bones lie like boulders, immobile? How does one who cannot move anything himself manage the most basic of human needs, the need to remove toxic waste from one's own body? The truth is that this is a messy and depressing, yet life-saving business. The spinal cord injury world calls it bowel training.

Every second night, the wait for the aide was one of serious anxiety for Mel. The indignity of the aide rapidly removing his regular clothes and then dressing him in a hospital gown – the attire of a patient – the insertion of the suppository, the wait for his body to react, the reliance on the aide to come often to check, and, once things were done, quickly clean him up nearly brought Mel to his virtual knees again and again. Resignation was not part of Mel's vocabulary, so he withstood it all and prayed fervently for recovery.

The indignities didn't end there. Heavy boots were placed on his feet in order to keep them flexed and his ankles fixed in place. Mel couldn't move his feet once the boots were fastened. In fact, he was unable to move his legs at all, once they were arranged in the bed. He was rolled onto his side, sometimes even to the side of his choice, and his legs were then bent, hips flexed, and legs positioned one in front of the other. Then the bed would be raised so that his upper body was more upright and his head was propped up with a few pillows. The pillow arrangement and head placement were particularly painful. Since the surgeries were still very recent, Mel had a huge and very uncomfortable neck brace digging into him from all angles. It took many attempts to try to get him into the best position, and this often exasperated the aides – and Mel – to their breaking points. I was often close to tears (I was not the only one) as I tried to help and come up with the right configuration of pillows (one thicker, one thinner, folded once, sideways, not the thick one; the thin one worked yesterday...) that made my poor husband moderately comfortable the last time. It was daily torture.

But there were some calmer days when Duronte the Aide Supreme was on duty. Duronte was a gift. His caring and reassuring attitude eased the indignities, but it was his understanding of just how to position Mel that gained him Mel's eternal gratitude. Duronte knew exactly how to place Mel's legs, the perfect height for the bed, the exact types of pillows and folds, and most amazingly, he did it all with efficiency and a smile. Even when Duronte was not assigned as Mel's aide, I would run to find out if he was on duty that evening and ask him to come help. Duronte's talent was truly a gift. I studied Duronte's placements with a critical eye, but to my dismay I never could quite duplicate what he did.

On the unfortunate days that Duronte was not on duty or the assigned aide had not managed to provide minimally adequate positioning for Mel, I would continue to attempt the almost impossible task of finding a comfortable position. It was imperative for me to succeed so that Mel would not be miserable for hours. How could I leave him like that?

"I think Duronte used an orange pillow yesterday folded in half and then one of the yellow ones. I'm sure of it."

"That doesn't feel right. It's all wrong," Mel would reply sadly.

"I'm sorry. Maybe they took the pillows away and brought new ones. They sure look like the ones from last night," I said, frantically looking around for other pillows.

"Maybe the bed is too high."

"Okay. I'll try lowering it a bit," I said, moving to the side of the bed and pressing the down button a little bit.

"No, no... that's all wrong!"

Covering my eyes and taking a deep breath, I said, "Okay. Let's start again."

And it would begin again. And again – until finally I would make progress or Mel became too exasperated.

Mel was completely worn out at the beginning of this process, and by the end it was with profound relief that his nighttime sleeping pills kicked in and he fell into a sleep of pure exhaustion. For a few hours, anyway....

And my nighttime routine?

I went home, checked the mail, answered messages, paid the bills and wrote the nightly blog. Sleep eventually found me as well – sometimes.

Making it Happen

Day 40

June 12, 2013

I find myself explaining Mel's recovery as a rebuild of his entire body starting with breathing and moving from there. Each and every muscle has to be rebuilt. Today I realized how accurate I have been. I watched Mel painstakingly write his name in block letters using the muscles of his fingers and wrists associated with fine motor skills. His accomplishment using his now weaker hand (the right) was truly remarkable. Just four weeks ago, his right hand barely moved! We had rejoiced when we saw his thumb move a fraction of an inch.

Day 41

June 13, 2013

Mel's favorite nurse Nicole came on shift tonight and echoed Mel's sentiments of the day when she told him that the staff was all abuzz because Mel had such a wonderful day. This is an incredible facility, and Mel continues to make progress here every day. The staff truly cares – and it makes a difference. Mel continues to be in excellent spirits, ever thankful to Hakadosh Baruch Hu.

Please continue in your tefillot and learning that his progress should continue until a full recovery. Everything is possible!

Standing

"You need to stand before you can walk," Beth said to Mel. "Tomorrow we're going to try a standing apparatus."

One of the challenges of being vertical after horizontal for extended time is that standing can cause a drop in blood pressure. The body is not used to working so hard to bring the blood to the brain. This is termed orthostatic hypotension.

Beth strapped Mel into the seat of the standing frame and helped him place his arms on the table top portion which had a cut out for his chest. He watched as she walked around to press the on button. Slowly, the chair-like contraption rose unfolding his body from a seated position to an upright position. Completely supported by the standing apparatus, he looked around the gym for the first time in months from his 5' 9" vantage. "Whoa!" he said. "This is great!"

Seconds later, it was over. The machine lowered him back down.

"Three minutes is more than I expected to try today," Beth stated.

"When can we do this again?" Mel asked.

"Tomorrow. We'll go for a bit longer then."

***

The next day, Mel rolled himself close to the standing frame and anxiously waited for Beth to strap him in and get him upright. Once again the machine moved and his body rose.

Oh no, I thought. I watched as Mel grasped at the table. He didn't look good.

161

Beth quickly pressed the down button.

"Your blood pressure dropped," she explained as she monitored his parlor and breathing for several minutes.

I could see by his face that he wanted to scream with frustration. After the resounding success and buoyancy of Day 1, he was catapulted back into reality as he slowly recovered from the effects of the rapid drop in blood pressure. Had he just hit the wall on recovery? Would he never be able to stand or walk?

"Beth," Mel said, "please promise me that we can try this again tomorrow. I don't want to give up on the ultimate goal of walking out of here."

"Of course we'll try again. I want you to walk out of here too."

With her assurance, Mel put the failure to the side but waited impatiently to prove that he could do it. He had to put it out of his mind, because if he let it consume him, he would expend precious energy on wasteful worry. He knew and later told me that this would not be productive. He needed all his strength to reach the next goal. He couldn't let the roller coaster of recovery mess with his brain.

***

Two long days later, Beth rolled him toward the standing frame. "I can do this!" he told her.

Carefully monitoring his blood pressure, Beth watched the minutes tick away and Mel stood – head held high – for 20 minutes – way past Beth's planned timeframe!

"It figures," Beth cheered, "you are such a showoff!"

Days 42-44

June 16, 2013

Friday was a good day. Beth, Mel's PT, had a goal of seven minutes in the standing apparatus, so Mel was still standing after 20 minutes! Just a little insight into Mel's work ethic and determination. He is a favorite with all the therapists that work with him. This was the first Shabbat since the accident that felt a bit like Shabbat. Mel truly enjoyed all his favorite Shabbat foods and was able to partake of the bread for HaMotzei. Also the weather was very cooperative, and we enjoyed a long siesta outside on the beautiful grounds here at Kernan.

Each day brings improvement and thank Hashem Mel continues to have a very positive outlook. Please continue to keep him in your tefillot and learning.

Sensitive and Graphic – Caution

There is a very sensitive area in the mess of spinal cord injury that is spoken about in hushed voices outside of the clinical setting. When one suffers a spinal cord injury that affects the sacral region of the spinal cord, there is a good chance that the injured will have grave difficulty with bladder, bowel and sexual function.

In yoga, this is the area associated with the second chakra, the seat of passion and pleasure. It is the area that affects our feelings, emotions, security, intimacy and connection. It is the seat of our basic functioning, our most intimate functioning.

Put this on the list of things you never thought to know until you know.

In other words, ignorance is bliss.

Our bliss was shattered on a sunny day in early July. The bladder specialist at the hospital had ordered a urodynamic procedure. Having met with the doctor briefly a few days before, we knew that the test would evaluate Mel's bladder functioning; his emptying and flow. I don't think either one of us had any reservations. In fact, I think we were hoping the doctors would remove the internal catheter and bag and Mel would gain more freedom. The bag often impeded progress during physical therapy sessions; its disconnection a constant worry when Mel was moved on and off the therapy tables as well as between exercises. Removal of the bag would be a great boon, and we were all about forward progress.

On the day of the procedure, I arrived after Mel had been taken to the office on the other side of the building. Expecting to be fairly early, I had taken my time and breezed through the front doors, my iPad in tow, thinking I would catch up on some emails while I waited in Mel's room.

I was intercepted in the lobby by one of Mel's nurses.

Mel will be right in," she said.

"Thanks. That was quick. I thought the procedure took at least an hour," I replied.

"It usually does, but they had to stop the procedure."

"Stop the procedure... Is Mel okay?"

"The doctor will be in to discuss it with both of you in a few minutes. Here comes Mel," she said.

What now? I thought desperately. Thinking back, I couldn't remember a time when Mel had not finished anything. Something must have gone terribly wrong. My heart sped up. I could feel it pounding in my chest.

Mel was rolled in on a gurney. He was clearly disturbed. His agitation seemed to increase as the nurse helped him into bed. *Bed in the middle of the day?* My own anxiety was rising as well. In minutes, the doctor walked in.

"Doctor, what happened?" I asked.

"I was afraid of this," he replied. "I've been watching Mel for a while now. He's been recovering so beautifully that I waited longer than usual to do this test. I see now that I was mistaken and should have been more proactive."

His apology was only confusing me and probably both of us, although so far Mel hadn't said anything.

"Mel wasn't able to handle the test. It was very distressing for him. His bladder is not emptying effectively, which means that he's at great risk for infection and for erosion of the bladder wall. He's already had some damage and we need to make immediate changes," he said pulling out some pictures of Mel's bladder and pointing to the area where the erosion had begun.

I looked at Mel, but he remained mute. "I don't understand," I said speaking for us. "I thought everything was fine; he had urine filling the bag all the time."

"Yes, but he's not emptying enough. His bladder's remaining filled at a dangerous level. We can't allow that to continue. He'll need to be catheterized every four hours."

"Doesn't he have a catheter now?"

"Yes, but this is different. The catheter he has now remains in place and catches the urine as it flows. Mel needs to be catheterized throughout the day to help his body empty. This is called intermittent catheterization."

"Is there a chance that he'll be able to empty better as he progresses?" I asked.

"Yes, there is always a chance," he said.

I detected a lack of conviction. My heart fell as I looked at Mel lying in the big hospital bed. He looked small and scared. Later, I would hear the sickening details of the failed procedure and realize the trauma he had experienced. I hadn't actually figured out what all this meant in a practical sense, but I knew this was a big step back in the progress department. We had hit our first real setback, and it was a game changer.

This setback was life-altering. It was all-consuming, and yet it was not something we could discuss with many outside the hospital. For days after this development, I found it extremely challenging to answer the constant inquiries concerning Mel's progress. It took us time to process and to accept.

After reading the Spinal Cord Injury Bible, a huge binder given to us by Kernan as a resource for all things Spinal Cord Injury, I discovered that the official name for Mel's issue of emptying incompletely is neurogenic underactive bladder. Neurogenic is the key term, because Mel had damage to the nerves governing the urinary tract. With my new understanding, I viewed the other patients at the hospital in a new light. I had felt sorry for the many, like Mel, that had urine bags hanging off their chairs. I had felt that the public display of their private functioning was somewhat embarrassing and sad. Instead, I reasoned that they were the lucky ones. Their systems were working with regularity, emptying and flowing properly. The patients without the urine bags were the questionable ones.

My ignorant reasoning turned out to be faulty, because I had over-simplified a much more complex issue. I had much to learn.

Without exception, the patients on Mel's unit were in their first stages of recovery. Many could not move their hands with much effectiveness. Most could not depend on their severely weakened or paralyzed legs to transfer to a toilet or stand to urinate. The challenges of those in the unit were humbling, and I wondered how many were dealing with the difficulties of the urinary system. My prayers encompassed the group. The meaning of Nurse Karen's words, "Everything below the point of injury is affected," became clearer. Yes, Karen. I thought. Now I'm beginning to understand.

Figuring out intermittent catheterization became our topmost priority. My only personal experience with catheters went back 25 years to the birth of our second daughter. Post-delivery, my nurse insisted that I urinate before allowing me to rest in bed. With her assistance in the bathroom, I made a good attempt. Unfortunately, I fainted, and when I came to found myself lying on the hospital bed looking up into the anxious eyes of the nurse.

"We'll need to catheterize you. Is that what you want?" she asked.

Although her tone was threatening, her expression exuded compassion.

Ignorant of what it meant to be catheterized and unsure what I could do to avoid it from my post-faint position, my reply was somewhat flippant.

"I guess you need to do what you need to do."

I had survived the catheterization, and I had no residual memories of how it felt. I figured Mel would manage as well.

As we worked through this formidable challenge, I noticed an upside to this despairing situation. Mel experienced increased freedom. Without the bag disconnecting and being a general nuisance as he moved through his PT exercises, his work progressed unhindered. Valuable therapy minutes weren't wasted as nurses were called to reconnect tubes. In addition, hydrotherapy in the pool was only possible because he did not have a bag. It was during hydrotherapy that Mel had his first taste of the possibility of standing.

Learning and mastering the technique of intermittent catheterization was the epitome of frustration. As we neared the date of Mel's expected release from the hospital, our anxiety over this challenge grew exponentially. Mel's fingers remained contracted, weak and ineffective for the fine motor manipulation needed for catheterization.

The hospital staff decided that if Mel couldn't do it, then I should. I was given a crash course. Unfortunately, it was a "show you once and now it's your turn" kind of instruction. Regrettably, Mel had a particularly ornery nurse the first few days of my "training." There was no sympathy from that corner.

"He's going home soon; you have to be able to do this," she insisted. "Call me if you have trouble."

Trouble, I thought. I could easily maim him for life! Clueless but determined, Mel and I put our heads together, worked step and by step and painstakingly figured it out. Once we did, the nursing staff announced that all day catheterizations would now be up to us to handle on our own. This meant that I needed to be at the hospital every four hours during the daytime, which was not a tenable situation. At this point in Mel's recovery, I was trying to fit in a few work hours after lunch and during his afternoon therapy session. Feeling grateful and blessed, I viewed my flexible job as a Database Administrator and Specialist for the State of Maryland with new appreciation. Extremely lucky to have amazingly understanding superiors and co-workers, as well as enough seniority and accrued hours, I was able to retain my job and our health benefits.

Keeping in touch with work daily, I strung together hours here and there throughout the first post-accident months to handle the most urgent of issues. Just a quick fifteen-minute drive from Kernan, I had recently begun to cobble together a few hours a day at the office. This every four-hour time constraint now brought a halt to those office runs. How would I ever leave Mel's side? I worried.

Frantic, I appealed to the urologist on staff, the one who had performed the failed procedure, and determined the need for intermittent catheterization. I described Mel's difficulty handling the catheters, specifically the limitations of his fingers and hands. Immediately receptive, he brought us a variety of different catheters to test.

Alone in Mel's hospital room, we tried each type of catheter.

"This thing is a life-saving tool," I reminded him holding a catheter in the air. "We must do this."

It was frightening and painful, but we found a type of catheter that Mel could manage himself. With tears and frustration, grit and determination, a method was found and life progressed. Check one off for the good guys.

Home Visit

The big day had finally arrived. Mel was coming home! It was only for a visit, but it meant that we were getting very close to the real thing. Mel and I waited expectantly in the front lobby for Beth and Lauren. We watched staff and patients come and go, the place a hive of activity.

"Beth should be here in just a minute," Lauren said as she approached. "She forgot something and ran back to the PT area. I'll see you at your house. Beth will come with me after she helps Mel into your car," she said before she headed to her car parked in the employee parking lot.

In the meantime Mel and I made our way outside. As I pushed his wheelchair through the automatic sliding doors, we were met by a muggy blast of over 100-degree heat. The Baltimore humidity is legendary, and that day was no exception. The thickness of the heat instantly made us sweat.

"It's hot as hell today," Mel said.

"It sure is. I'll put on the air as soon as we get in the car," I replied.

Beth soon emerged with a clipboard and a wooden transfer board. She waited with Mel while I brought his gray Honda Accord to the front. I made sure to leave the car running with the air conditioner on full blast.

The process of getting Mel into the car was one we had practiced several times before in preparation for this very day. Beth watched as I took the side arm off of Mel's wheelchair and positioned the chair by the open passenger door, the seat of the wheelchair in line with the car seat. Mel helped by lifting himself up a bit, while I slid the transfer board underneath his backside, the open end reaching across to the car seat. Expertly, Mel slid himself along the board with me positioned in front of him to help if necessary. My hovering hands never touched him. The smile on his face was one of success. He had done the transfer without any assistance. This was a big deal, something we had hoped and prayed would be possible. Beth and I looked like proud mommies ourselves as we smiled and nodded.

Beth went to find Lauren. I closed Mel's door, ran around to close mine and then made my way to the trunk where I dismantled the wheelchair with somewhat less efficiency than I would in later days. Wheelchair assembly is an art form to be mastered. I took off the remaining armrest, then the cushions, backrest and seat; next the leg rests, and finished with the wheels. Finally I folded and stored the frame of the chair along with all the parts in the trunk. I closed the trunk with a resounding thud and made my way to the driver's seat.

"That was fast," Mel said, complimenting me on my mechanical skills.

"Not too bad. I'm getting the hang of it. Here we go," I said, turning the key. "Homeward bound!"

We settled in for the 25-minute ride.

"So, this is the way I go every day. They were doing some construction here last month, but thankfully that's finished," I said.

"And here's the golf course," I said after another minute or so. "There are people out here all day long crossing the road in their golf carts. They zip around and even cross the street in their carts."

Noticing how quiet Mel was, I looked over at him. He didn't look happy or excited. We were on our own for the first time in two and a half months, and I was so hyped, eager for him to see the house again. It suddenly dawned on me that he was probably worried and apprehensive.

"Yael should be there when we get home. She said she'll meet us there," I said to cheer him.

No answer. He was miles away, so we drove the rest of the way in silence. Fearing it was sensory overload for him just being in the car and out of the hospital, I didn't even put on the radio. Worry began to nag at me. *I don't know about this. I hope it's going to be okay*, I thought.

Pulling into our driveway, I said, "Look everyone's here, honey." Yael, Beth and Lauren were waiting for us on the front lawn with big smiles of welcome on their faces. "The house is just as you left it."

"Hi everyone," I said as I got out of the car. Opening the trunk, I quickly put the wheelchair back together as Yael went around to Mel's side to greet him. Frame, leg rests, cushions back and seat, then right armrest. The sun beat down on us as Mel made another great transfer, and I slid the left armrest in place.

Wheeling Mel to the front steps, five in number, we all looked at the steps with optimism. Beth had been training Mel on the method needed to make his way up those steps. I had measured their width and rise and reported to her the week before, and she had geared Mel's step training to the exact measurements. They had worked very hard., because steps were one of our biggest issues for homecoming.

Yael and I watched expectantly as Mel attempted the first step. Mel held the left-hand railing and Beth assisted him from his right side. It was immediately apparent that both Beth and Lauren were needed, because Mel could not find enough strength in his left knee and leg to lift it to the step and gain purchase. A previous ACL surgery on that knee rendered it weaker and less functional that we had hoped. Our two heroic therapists virtually lifted Mel up those five steps, one gigantic hurdle at a time.

Overheated and exhausted, Mel dropped into the wheelchair Yael had carried up the steps and positioned on the porch for him. As I rolled him into the house, we were a subdued group.

The house was as hot as an oven. I had simply failed to set the air conditioner early enough in the day for it to cool the house off by the time we arrived. Noted by all, I apologized over and over, but that didn't make Mel any more comfortable. His autonomic nervous system was still not operating optimally, also compromised by the injury, and I think he felt the heat much more intensely than did the rest of us. I rolled him into the kitchen, put the overhead fan on high, brought everyone cold drinks, and left Yael and Mel to visit while Beth and Lauren joined me for the house assessment.

Until Mel's accident, getting up and down stairs in our split-level house was never problematic. As we approached homecoming, the structural formation was way up there on my list of worries. It seemed there were stairs everywhere. Short flights, but to reach the essentials – kitchen, bathroom, bedroom – at least one group of six steps must be traversed.

The three of us made our way up the stairs to our makeshift master bedroom.

"I'm so relieved that our friend Gary found us chair lifts, one for this flight and one for the stairs to the den on the lower level," I rambled on excitedly to Beth and Lauren. "I was amazed that he found them. He contacted a charitable organization in our community and they located two useable chair lifts that can be adapted to our configuration. I'm so grateful and excited. I was afraid we would need to find another place to live, because stairs are such an issue. I really wasn't sure what we would do."

"That's great news. From what I can see so far, you're right. It would not have been doable on a long-term basis," Beth said.

"Friends keep suggesting we move into an apartment or a condo. I don't know how I could have arranged all that before Mel's discharge. And it would be so sad for us. This has been our home for 25 years. Of course, if it's necessary, I'll figure it out."

"You're doing a great job, Judy. It looks like you won't have to find another place to live. This should work for you, at least for a while," Lauren said.

The ladies quickly looked over the hall bathroom and found no issues. As we backtracked to our temporary master bedroom, we passed yet another staircase heading upward. Our master bedroom lay behind the closed door. Briefly, I wondered if Mel and I would ever share that precious space again. Shaking my head, I listened as Beth and Lauren discussed the doorways; the one into the bedroom and the one to the attached bathroom. Thankfully, the doorways were wide enough for the wheelchair, but the bathroom door in the bedroom would need to be removed to make space for the wheelchair to roll far enough inside. My brother Harry would be my go-to person for the door. One call from me, and the door would be gone. In the bathroom, we discussed the need for a bath chair and a raised toilet seat. I would find those items in short order. They were not hard to get.

Leaving the bathroom, Beth said, "It would be a good idea to lower the bed height by removing the bed frame." She lifted up the brown and white comforter atop the bed and pointed to the simple metal bed frame. "It'll be easier for Mel to transfer without the frame."

"Looking good," Lauren said with a thumbs up as we left the bedroom and made our way downstairs.

Immediately, Lauren noticed the area rugs, one by the door and one in the living room. "All rugs need to be removed," she said. "Too difficult for wheelchairs."

"Of course," I agreed, putting all my amateur interior decorator notions firmly aside. I had spent many hours choosing those living room area rugs, something to bring the colors together. But home décor was certainly no longer a consideration when accessibility was paramount. Bare bones it would be, like our lives at this time.

Mel and Yael joined us in the living room, and Mel transferred to the taupe leather sofa by the far wall. It was heartwarming to see him again on our couch in our house, albeit a bit stiff looking. In fact, he sat in almost the exact same position on the sofa as the day of his fateful ride, the last moment I had seen him in our home, our last moment here together before the accident. Transported back to May 3, I remembered the way his head was cocked slightly sideways as he spoke to our daughter Shana. As I waved goodbye on the way to my yoga class, I listened to him give Shana a special Shabbat blessing. Whispering "Amen", I pulled the door closed behind me, not knowing how significant that moment would be, how much I would yearn for his homecoming and to see him again in that very spot.

While I was busy with my thoughts and their pull on my heartstrings, Lauren and Beth proceeded to assess our kitchen. For accessibility, they suggested that I move some of the dishes and cooking utensils into the lower cabinets. For closer access, they suggested I find a workman to pull out the cabinet below the sink.

We'll write up a full list for you," Lauren said.

"That's a great idea," I said. From our discussion, the list would be far smaller than I had imagined and with no major financial outlay. I had feared that the structural changes alone would be in the tens of thousands of dollars. Relieved, I realized that everything could be assembled and completed in the small timeframe we had, just two short weeks. The assessment had been a great success. I had my working orders.

"This sofa isn't really comfortable, I seem to be sliding," Mel said. "Can someone help me back into the chair?"

Four pairs of eyes zoned in on Mel. He had slid significantly, his legs far forward and his back and neck at an odd angle.

Quickly, Yael grabbed his chair and I helped him transfer back into it. Then, Yael rolled him onto the porch. She waited with Mel, talking quietly, as Beth, Lauren and I figured out the ramp situation, the last item on the assessment checklist.

In order to conform to the guidelines set by the Americans with Disabilities Act, ramps must extend one foot in length per height inch to maintain a safe angle of elevation. Therefore our porch height required a 30-foot ramp. After much thought, I believed that the ramp would extend from the rightmost side of our porch and flow down our driveway alongside our house. I was prepared for our porch railing to be dismantled or cut to allow for the ramp. Luckily, Beth had a better plan.

"If you take the ramp through your back screened-in porch and then turn it toward the driveway, you'll still have room to park and will have more than enough footage to make a nice smooth incline," she suggested.

Lauren and I quickly agreed, nodding. "That will save my porch railing and still allow me to park in the driveway. Great!" I said enthusiastically.

"That's it for the assessment. Do you think you can get the things we discussed done in the next few weeks?"

"I think so," I replied. "Our friend Gary has already found the two chair lifts and the installers. He also found someone to build the ramp. All the rest I can handle." Silently I thanked Gary once again for being there for us and for finding solutions even before I asked.

We looked at Mel and Yael on the porch.

"How are we going to get Mel back down?" I asked.

"We'll manage," Beth said looking at Lauren.

Together they did manage. Yael and I hovered nearby as they literally carried Mel and the heavy wheelchair down the five steps. The ramp was definitely on the "To Do Immediately" list.

"Okay, we're good to go. I'll write up the list for you," Lauren said after she caught her breath.

They watched as Yael rolled Mel over to the passenger side of his car. "Bye, honey," Mel said as she stepped back. "Thanks so much for coming home to be with me for the visit."

"No problem, Dad. I'll see you at the hospital soon." Yael was true to her word. She made numerous visits to the hospital throughout the almost three months of Mel's inpatient recovery. She was there at least once every week. Her visits were always welcome, always helpful, and always left us with more strength to continue.

I put the transfer board in place and positioned myself to assist. Once again Mel made another flawless transfer. He didn't need my help.

Beth and Lauren rode away, waving.

After Mel was buckled, I set to work taking apart the wheelchair and storing it in the trunk. I hugged Yael, "Thanks, honey. It was great that you were here with us. Love you tons."

The home visit was over. Yael drove back to school and we went back to the hospital. Mel's homecoming was coming into focus.

It's Time

"He needs all the therapy he can get," Gary insisted.

"I think so too, but he's acting like a patient, like he's sick and unable to do," I tried explaining. The compassion in Gary's deep-set eyes was all the answer I was going to get.

"He can do more now," I continued. "He regresses when he gets back into bed at the end of the day. I need to get him out of here."

Gary had been advocating for continued inpatient therapy as Mel's discharge date grew closer. The doctors and staff had been preparing us for Tuesday, July 30, only a week away, but Gary wanted more time for his dear friend.

"If insurance won't pay, we can raise money to cover the costs. Just give me the word and I'll set it in motion. Only the best for Mel."

"I know. I think so too, but I don't think inpatient is right for him anymore. Don't ask for donations now. Let's wait. Maybe he'll need a different type of therapy or something else later on. He needs to get home and start realizing that he can do more than he thinks."

I had been watching Mel; the understatement of the year. I had watched every single move he had made for the past three months. In awe, I watched him rebuild, and I watched him fight the incredible fight with unparalleled determination. I watched the balance shift. Instead of being unable to move and needing all possible help, he was growing stronger and more able to do things on his own. As Mel often said, "I am injured, not sick."

In the past week or so, I had noticed an attitude shift, very subtle at first. During the day, Mel would use his hands and his new muscle strength, demonstrating marked independence. But in the evening, he was suddenly unable to do the tasks he had previously mastered. Docilely, he succumbed to letting the nurses and aides move him at their will, without his physical or verbal input. This was very different from being a patient and needing help. The change was gradual but noticeable to me. I watched the nurses turn him side to side. "You can turn yourself now," I told him repeatedly. "You can press the button to raise and lower the bed to make yourself more comfortable." Shaking my head, I watched the independence he displayed by day turn to dependence on the nursing staff at night. Some of that resistance could be chalked up to end-of-day fatigue. I suppose I could have left things alone with just shy of a week to go, but my uneasiness was growing. He was fighting valiantly for his autonomy, and I wouldn't let him slide on my watch. My other reasoning was not so altruistic. Who was going to turn him at home?

Worried, I approached Dr. Y., Mel's primary rehabilitation physician and a gifted physiastrist, outside the gym on Thursday. "Do you think it would be all right to take Mel home a bit early?" I asked him. "I really feel that he needs to go home and start living."

"Yes. Absolutely," he agreed readily. "I think you're right. He's done amazingly well and will continue to improve in outpatient therapy. I think he's definitely ready."

"Really?" I asked stunned.

"Yes. Mel's ready. It's time."

"Can we start outpatient Monday, so he won't miss any therapy? I don't want him to lose momentum."

"Sure. I can arrange that. I'll set up the discharge for tomorrow afternoon. He can have his regular therapy as scheduled and then you can take him home after. I'll notify his outpatient therapists and set up times for him to begin on Monday. He won't miss anything." I was aware that this was not the regular course of things. The normal protocol was for patients to go home for a few weeks and have in-home therapy a few times a week as they adjusted to the home environment. Then, if ready, they would proceed to outpatient therapy.

"That sounds amazing. He's really okay to go?"

"He is. You're doing the right thing Judy. You've been an outstanding advocate for him."

I thanked Dr. Y., my head spinning. I knew it, I thought. I knew it was time! Pumping my fists in the air, I allowed myself an expression of euphoria. I was getting him out of there. To boot, I had just saved us another grueling Shabbat at Kernan.

My celebration was short-lived, my fists falling to my sides as the scary truth hit full force. Within twenty-four hours we would be on our own.

Dr. Y. set all the wheels in motion and I relayed the news to Mel.

"We're going to do great," I said, trying to convince myself.

"Yes we are!" Mel agreed. He didn't need convincing.

Homecoming

As Beth and I watched Mel take a few steps with his shiny new walker, she handed me a pristine transfer board. His last inpatient therapy session was almost over. Mel was actually coming home, not in weeks, not in days, but in minutes. Luckily, I was not hooked up to a heart rate monitor. I'm not sure anyone would have let us go.

All the wheels were in motion. I prayed that the ramp leading from our driveway to the back door was finished. A local contractor, Ari, had agreed to build and install the wooden ramp, generously donating his time and effort. He had agreed to build the ramp in the original timeframe, but that had been moved up by a few precious days. Gary had coordinated the effort, assuring me that Ari would take care of it. "Don't worry," he had said. Easier said than done. Unfortunately for me, Gary and Sherri were off in Italy on vacation, Ari had not finished before I left for Kernan that morning, and I was biting my nails.

The downstairs ramp also had me sweating. At ten the night before, I had arrived home withered with exhaustion. Before I had even put my pocketbook down, I blinked to make sure I was seeing straight. A huge six-inch metal rail lay diagonally across the entrance to the kitchen, blocking it. "Oh My God!" I shouted to the empty house. "What have they done?" I ran around to the dining room side of the kitchen and assessed. I stared at the threshold strip. Made of thick wood, it would be a hassle to traverse. The hardwood floor installer had created a makeshift strip that sat much higher than normal transition strips. I thought about getting Mel in his wheelchair over that bulky divider between kitchen and dining room. "No good," I ground my teeth, trying to keep the tears at bay.

Fumbling for my phone in my pocketbook, I called our friend Craig, Gary's backup, as I slumped on the stairs leading to the bedrooms.

"The ramp is blocking the kitchen," I tried to explain to Craig. "It's enormous and ends right in the middle of the kitchen doorway. There is no way to get the wheelchair past it. Why did they leave it like this?"

"Wait a minute, Judy. Calm down. Who did what?" Craig asked again.

"The people who installed the chair rail. I guess it's too long, but it ends right in the middle of the kitchen doorway – blocking it! I'll never be able to get Mel's wheelchair around it. It's so in the way. I'll probably kill myself on it. It's huge!"

"Who's doing the installing?"

"I thought you knew," I said, thinking hard. "I think it's CHAI (Comprehensive Housing Assistance Incorporated). What did Gary say?" I continued thinking out loud.

"I'll make some calls," Craig said. "Don't worry. We'll get them to fix it."

"By tomorrow?"

"Yes. By tomorrow. I'll figure it out."

"I know you must think I'm nuts. But if you saw it, you'd understand. I'm sorry to bother you so late and in such a panic."

"Hang in there. It's going to be fine. Really. We'll fix this."

Hanging up, I suddenly remembered the contact name at the charity organization. Running downstairs I grabbed the community directory from the table in the den and dialed. I didn't waste a minute before calling, to hell with the time, politeness, or anything else. What a mess!

The kind coordinator picked up immediately. "I'm so sorry the workmen left it like that for you. I'll get them to remove it first thing tomorrow."

"That would be great. I don't know how we can manage the way it is."

"Of course not. We may not be able to get it installed tomorrow. I'm not sure how far they'll get before you come home, but I'll make sure they finish first thing Monday."

Relieved, I hung up and immediately called Craig back and brought him up to speed.

"It's going to be okay," I said to myself as I maneuvered past the rail and went into the kitchen.

***

"It's going to be okay," I reminded myself as we headed out of the gym, Mel waving to his friends, and the therapy staff on the way out. The last inpatient therapy session was on the books, and we were off.

"I just want to check your room one last time," I said pushing the wheelchair toward the reception desk. "I'll just be a minute. Okay?"

"Go ahead. I'm fine here," he replied.

I had emptied Mel's room and loaded all the assorted junk, food, and accumulated ridiculousness into the car prior to the therapy session, but my A-type personality wouldn't let me leave without a final check. As I entered the corner room for the last time, I felt the weeks deep in my bones. Had it really been nearly ten whole weeks since Shana and I waited in that empty room for Mel to show up? This space had been our entire existence for months. The room echoed with our heartache and worry, failure and triumphs. Images swirled in my mind as I quickly checked each drawer, counter and shelf.

At the doorway, I turned and swept the room with my eyes one last time. With a half-smile on my face, I walked out.

Mel expertly transferred to the passenger seat of the car.

"This is really it. It seems like a dream," he said.

Nodding, I started the engine. Twenty-five minutes later, we were home. I don't recall any specific conversation. We were each lost in our own thoughts.

"Welcome home," I said opening his door.

"Nice ramp," Mel said.

"Oh yay! Ari finished it! Thank God!"

"Good thing."

"Yeah it is. I'm not sure what we would've done. I guess Sammy would have helped. He's on his way," I said referring to my cousin Sammy, PT extraordinaire. When the official homecoming date changed, we opted to tell only a small number of people. Of course, Sammy was in the group. He and his wife Malka had prepared our temporary bedroom on the middle level, cleaning and straightening the embarrassingly messy space. Lovingly, they had taken the bed off the frame per Lauren's direction and installed handgrips and the raised toilet seat in the bathroom. "What can we do to help?" was their refrain.

Sammy had assured me that he would be there to help us settle in. Not only was he coming to make sure we could manage in the short term, but his son Elan had graciously volunteered to stay over the first night to make sure we were okay. Cousin Elan, handsome and capable, is a superb nurse in his own right. At Shock Trauma, Devon had reminded me so much of Elan with his dark hair, compact build, and direct and efficient manner. You knew you could trust either of them to have your back. That night Elan told us that he had been one of the first responders to Mel's accident. In the neighborhood at the time, he had heard the ambulances and had stopped to check on the injured man on the street. It wasn't until later, long after he had left the scene and Mel had been transported to Shock Trauma, that he realized the man lying face down was his own cousin, Mel.

The ramp was perfect. I pushed Mel easily up the ramp and across the short expanse of the porch to our back door. There was just one tricky moment, accompanied by a bit of labored breathing and the chair tilting precariously to get it over the uneven door lip, and we were in. Straight ahead, I noticed the path was clear to the living room, no railing extended diagonally. I breathed a sigh of relief. The village had come through again.

We had just made our way through the kitchen when I heard a knock on the door.

"That must be Sammy," Mel said.

"Right on time," I replied opening the door for Sammy. "We just got home."

"Welcome home, brother," Sammy said, gently slapping Mel on the back. "You want to take a ride?" he said motioning toward the chair lift leading up to the next level. The offending chair lift that had been obstructing the kitchen had been moved against the lower level far wall.

"Sure," Mel agreed readily. "Let's see how this thing works."

I watched as Sammy lowered the side rail on Mel's wheelchair and helped Mel transfer to the seat of the chair rail. Sammy strapped Mel in, as I looked around for the remote control. Finding it, I started to look it over.

"Ready?" Sammy asked, as he took the remote.

On Mel's nod, Sammy hit the button.

"It works!" I exclaimed, as the chair – with Mel in it – slowly ascended to the top of the six steps.

Sammy and I looked at Mel. So far so good. Or was it? All our smiles turned to frowns as our first glitch came into focus. Mel's seat was positioned too high off the ground. He was not at chair height. Earlier in the week, I had picked up two transport type wheelchairs at a local *Gemach*, a community-organized sharing service. I scrambled to get the chair I had waiting on the upper level.

"What are we going to do?" I asked, pushing the wheelchair next to Mel. Looking quickly at Sammy, I read the message in his eyes: "Don't panic, Judy, or I'll bop you over the head." I guess the squeak in my voice had tipped him off.

"I can stand," Mel said finding the solution.

"The walker," Sammy replied.

"Oh," I said running back down the stairs to get it. Walker, wheelchairs, bath seats, raised toilet seat, I had gathered all kinds of sundry accessories for Mel's homecoming.

Sammy carefully positioned the walker and Mel turned his body and angled it toward the waiting walker. Taking hold, he brought his feet down and stood.

"Mission accomplished!" he said with satisfaction. High-fiving, Sammy and I trailed behind as Mel walked the dozen or so steps into the waiting bedroom, the one he and Malka had prepared.

We had made it to the bedroom. Mel moved to the side of the bed and sat down. "Wow, Sammy, I'm glad you were here for that!" I exclaimed.

Moving around to the far side of the bed, Sammy told Mel, "I'm not through with you yet. I want to see how you'll get up off that bed. Lay down."

Mel stretched out on the bed. "Now roll toward me and show me how you'll get up." With great effort, Mel rolled somewhat onto his side. Attempting to swing his legs over proved too much for his weakened core.

Noting the difficulty, Sammy planted Mel's right elbow and forearm on the bed. "Use your arm to help you," he urged, pressing the forearm down.

Mel's arm lost purchase and he flopped down. Determined, he re-planted his forearm and pressed into it. Rolling side to side, he gained momentum. It took multiple attempts, but finally his legs cleared the bed and he was propelled to a seated position.

"Good. That's good. Try again," Sammy directed.

Mel stretched out again, took a few breaths, planted his arm, and began again. After fewer attempts, and with better momentum and more control, he swung to a seated position.

"Excellent," Sammy said, smiling. "You can do it. That was very good. I wasn't sure how that would go." His eyes met mine and I sent him a silent thank you, realizing how significant this moment was and how much more independence Mel would have with this task on his "I can do it" list.

"Elan will be here after dinner. Do you need anything before I go?" he asked.

"I don't think so. But I guess we'll find out soon enough," I replied.

"We'll be fine. It's really good to be home," Mel said.

"It's good to have you home. No more five mile hikes for me," he said, referring to the incredible effort he and Malka made to trek the distance to visit us a few of the Shabbat afternoons early on at Kernan. "Let's get you back down the steps and make sure the chair lift works in that direction before I go."

I brought the walker close to the bed and once again Sammy and I followed Mel down the hallway.

Reversing the process, Mel eased into the chair lift seat from a standing position. This time, I strapped him in and pressed the button. At the bottom of the steps, Mel transferred to the waiting wheelchair. There was no height issue on that end.

"Well done, well done. Shabbat Shalom.   I'll see you Sunday," Sammy said walking to the front door.

"Thanks, Sam. Really appreciate everything," Mel said.

"So glad to see you home, my friend," he replied, waving. "Call me if you need anything."

I followed Sammy outside and thanked him then slowly closed the door.

"You're really home!   I can barely believe it," I said with a big grin on my face.

"Neither can I," he replied. "I'm kinda tired. I think I'll take a rest here," he said rolling the chair farther into the living room.

"Not sure why you're tired, you lazy bum," I said smiling. "Good. You rest, and I'll get dinner ready."

Hours later, the Shabbat candles glowed in the corner of the kitchen. Standing, Mel braced himself on his walker with one hand and held the glass Kiddush cup aloft in the other. By his side, my gaze traveled from Mel's beautiful, triumphant smile to the colorful stemmed wineglass in his hand. This was the tenth week, the tenth Shabbat since Mel's transfer to Kernan. The unbelievable had happened. We were home – different, changed in so many ways – but returned to our environment, to our home, to each other. I placed the tenth plastic cup on a shelf in the cupboard, noting that the last and final cup in the package had not survived unscathed, much like us. It was cracked and unusable as a cup, although as a reminder of all we had to be grateful for, it was a unique shining symbol.

Mel recited the blessing over the wine, his voice strong, although tinged with emotion. With jerky yet functional movements, he brought the wineglass to his lips and took a sip. After he swallowed, he extended the glass toward me. I reached over to take it. Moments passed as his fingers slowly opened enough to release the wineglass into my hand. We both waited patiently. Spasticity remained. There was still a considerable amount of healing to look forward to but we refused to let the negative steal our joy. I took a sip of wine, savoring its sweetness and the sweetness of the moment.

Our first meal home together, our first Shabbat meal, truly was a singular event. Mel was back. Shabbat was back. The food tasted delicious, the house warm and inviting, life full of possibilities. It was one of those times in life when one is aware and fully cognizant that this is a special moment, a moment that will be remembered, a moment that resonates deep into the soul and makes one a believer.

Elan arrived shortly after dinner. He visited with us for a short time and then helped Mel get ready for bed. Exhausted and with the aid of sleeping pills, Mel was asleep quickly. I followed soon enough. Mel was home, lying by my side. The world had finally righted itself.

Outpatient Therapy

I wheeled Mel into a temporary therapy gym, because a complete renovation of the outpatient side of the Kernan gym was started over the weekend. The small space was filled with therapy tables and physical therapy parallel bars. He was ready to meet his new therapists and anxious to get going after a successful first weekend at home.

Days 87-88

July 30, 2013

Mel is back in the saddle. He had his initial evaluations with his new primary OT (Heather) and PT (Tasha) therapists. He demonstrated all his new capabilities and we await the new bar that each will set for his progress.

Mel went back to Shock Trauma for his neurosurgery follow-up appointment. The cervical collar that has been a source of discomfort for the past twelve weeks is finally history (but not so distant a memory yet)!

Upward and onward as Mel continues to gain stamina and strength while enjoying the view from our own front porch.

Wheelchair Outing

"Let's go out for a while," Mel said.

"Sure. It'll be great to get out of the house," I replied clearing the lunch dishes. "Just give me a few more minutes to finish up here and then I'll grab my hat."

"I'll help you as much as I can," Mel said. "I know that pushing me in the wheelchair will be hard for you."

"I'll be fine. Don't worry," I said, knowing that I would manage and understanding how emotionally important it was for Mel to contribute. He wanted desperately to be more independent with his mobility, but his arm strength was severely lacking. Although the muscles were building, progress was at a snail's pace. It was problematic for him to grasp the wheels sufficiently, plus the protective gloves he needed to wear reduced the minimal sensation he had. The difficulties were often overwhelming.

As we made our way out through the back porch and down the new ramp, Mel repeated, "I'll help you as much as I can."

"I know you will, and I know whatever you can do will be a big help to me," I said, sincerely hoping that he would be able to for his own sake.

We rolled along the sidewalk and around the block. Mel worked very hard, concentrating with every step. I could feel his tension and his effort.

"Take a break," I said. "The pavement is flat and I'm doing fine. You've given me good momentum."

"All right," he said panting. "Just for a few minutes."

It was a sunny day during the first week of August and luckily it wasn't too hot or sticky. Baltimore summers are usually brutal. But on this day we were both happy to be out and about, away from hospitals, on our own. It was a joy that I hoped we could embrace every day to come, a joy that I hoped we would never take for granted.

We rounded another corner and came to a curb, a regular curb with no gradation. I stopped and went around the chair to assess.

"I don't think I can bump you down this curb, honey," I said, facing him, my hands gravitating to my hips. "It's too big, and I'm afraid I won't be able to control the chair."

"I don't want you to hurt yourself. Let's turn around," he said, just as a young acquaintance and her sister called out to us. One of them lived in the apartments adjacent to the parking area we were facing. The curb led to the parking area.

We waved at the couple. "We seem to be a bit stuck," Mel said with a small smile.

"Do you want some help?" one of the girls asked.

"No, but thanks," Mel replied.

"We're lucky," I said leaning over to speak quietly in Mel's ear. "We don't need to go this way. We're just taking a walk. It's not a big deal for us. Let's just turn around and head the other way."

We chatted with the two girls across the parking lot for a few moments, waved goodbye and then turned around. As we started back, I wondered aloud, "What would we have done if we really needed to go that way?"

"I know. It's crazy," Mel said. "How many more curbs in the area are inaccessible?"

"I don't know. I sure will be checking it out from now on." What if Mel had been alone? I thought, cringing.

Exhausting himself, Mel helped me on the way back. Yet, as we pulled into our driveway he insisted on helping, his arms barely moving, as we made our way up the ramp, across the back porch and into the kitchen. I wheeled him into the living room and locked the chair.

"I need a big rest," he admitted as I handed him a glass of water.

"You sure do. You worked very hard."

"But I didn't really help very much, did I?" he said, taking a drink.

"Yes you did," I said with emphasis. "And you did much more than last time when we just went around our cul-de-sac. You're getting stronger. You just got home from the hospital. It's going to take some time."

"I know, I know. Can you help me get to the sofa?"

"Of course," I said taking his glass and placing it on the end table. After I lowered the side rail on his wheelchair, Mel transferred to the couch. I hovered, ready to help if needed.

I checked my watch. We had been gone 20 minutes.

Week 13

August 3, 2013

Home therapy is truly the best therapy. The transition to home has gone very well. It is remarkable how much progress can be made by doing one's daily activities in one's own environment. It has been wonderful to be home and to see Mel thrive. He is walking with his walker much more and with relative ease each day. He is managing more of his personal care and even helping me around the house! The chair lifts and ramp that were installed by the much appreciated efforts of Chai and Ari have made our home accessible. Mel transitions to the chairs with finesse.

Mel has settled into his new routine of outpatient therapy. He had productive sessions with his new OT, Heather, and his PT duo of Tasha and Bobbie. Outpatient therapy is different in focus and technique and Mel is adjusting to being included in the decisions of what to do each session. Basically, Heather is working on hand dexterity while Tasha and Bobbie are working on walking and stair preparation.

Mel must truly work hard every day, yet his spirit and determination remain steadfast. Please continue to daven for Mel. So much good has already come of the many prayers, tehillim and mitzvot with him in mind, and we are eternally grateful.

Engagement Party

I stood in the middle of our small cul-de-sac. Rotating counterclockwise, I examined each neighbor's house in turn for accessibility. How many steps to reach the front door? Were there railings to hold by the stairs? In reality, there are few home models represented in our development. "Boring", I would almost venture to say. Yet each home is unique in its accessibility from the street, each built with slightly different elevation. Some homes have more steps to the front door, some less. I approach each home in my mind and count the obstacles. I picture the inside floor plan of each home. Is there a bathroom on the first floor? Are there steps, area rugs, excess furniture that would be difficult to maneuver around with a wheelchair? Accessibility had become paramount in my consciousness. I again realize that you don't know to look for these things and fret over them until they become significant to you. Worry had become my middle name.

Mel was home. We were managing, actually doing nicely. We were enjoying the quiet and peace of our own space, and reveling in our private time together. But social being that he is, Mel was itching to get out. He needed his friends. He was determined, and he especially wanted to make it to the upcoming engagement party for Pam and Neil's daughter at their home. While Mel and I were immersed in recovery, Neil and Pam had somehow found the time and energy to be by our side and simultaneously pack up 22 years of their life and move to a beautiful new home. I wasn't sure how they had managed both with barely a complaint, and I was anxious to get a glimpse of their new abode.

We did the whole wheelchair, ramp, car, walker routine and Mel, Pam, and I stood outside the new house facing their kitchen door, the slightly more accessible of the two entrances. Three pairs of eyes assessed the five wooden steps with a wooden railing on each side, key to a successful entry. The sixth step, the one leading from porch level to kitchen entrance, was almost one and a half times the height of the other steps. Thinking of Mel's current level of progress, the incline looked like Mount Kilimanjaro to me.

"I can do it," Mel piped up. "I can."

"We'll help. I'll make sure we have a bunch of strong guys nearby," Pam replied.

"Okay," I said realizing I was the only member of the "Not Sure About This" club.

***

We returned two days later for the party. As Mel approached the steps, I think half the party streamed out the door. Soon there was quite a group assembled at the bottom of the steps surrounding Mel. After Mel grabbed the handrails, I moved the walker off to the side. With strong, able helpers in front and on each side, he started up the steps. I trailed behind, ready to push if need be. Pulling with his arms, he planted his right leg on the step and then slowly brought the left up to meet it. A collective sigh rose, as he made it up the first step. Continuing in this manner, right then left then stop, he traversed the first five steps. At the landing, he paused. Releasing his grip on the railings, he transferred his hands to the doorframes. He moved forward, two sets of strong arms lent him support from the sides and I pushed from the rear. A cheer resounded when he cleared the top step. It had truly taken the entire group to get him there, but we did it, and Mel triumphantly entered the kitchen.

Exhausted, smiling ear to ear, and supported by his walker, Mel moved toward the chair closest to the door. That day, he didn't venture further into the house, but there was no need. The party came to him. The beautiful bride, Maayan, and her adorable groom, Jeremy, were especially gracious and solicitous. Everyone was excited that Mel was there and he was not left alone for a single moment. With close friends and lots of love, Mel re-entered society. His non-wavering smile told the whole story.

Much later, when the party was over and Mel more than ready to go home, a small group helped him make his way down the stairs. Down was definitely different from up, both with their challenges. Carefully, he moved his left foot first down the step, his right down, and then stopped to adjust. Hands sliding along the railings, blood pumping, he made his way down, the group matching his pace. I thought of Beth at Kernan. Always honest, she had said, "I don't know if he'll be able to walk steps, Judy, it may not happen. We'll do everything we can to make it happen, but it may not. I really don't know."

Beth, I thought, I wish you were here. You would be so proud. I just witnessed true bravery, true grit and strong determination. I had just witnessed real success.

I took my hero home for a well-deserved rest. But guess what? He didn't stay for long. He insisted that we go to another engagement party later in the day. Thankfully, there were no steps involved. Steps had not been mastered by a long shot, but they had been successfully attempted. The homes of our friends and family were not totally off-limits. The revelation was freedom, removing some of the trapped feeling that I had tried not to let seep into my being.

Through his determination, Mel had literally taken his first baby steps.

Week 16 begins - Day 106

August 19, 2013

With great joy, I report that Mel is back in society! He made his way to shul this past Shabbat by wheelchair, but then used only a walker inside the building. Many thanks to Gary who gave me a break and pushed him back and forth. Mel efficiently and proudly walked his way to the center area and said the Gomel blessing. Immediately, he was surrounded by well-wishers. Rabbi Silber held his hand and danced with him as many sang and danced around them. The moment was truly transcendent and the joy of the kehillah palpable. Many tears of joy were shed as Mel rejoined the world.

One of the most unsettling things about the past three and a half months was the cessation of normal life and not being part of the happenings of our world. Life was simply day to day survival and complete focus on the insular happenings at Shock Trauma and then Kernan. Mel attended no minyanim, no shiurim, no smachot, no funerals. He did not eat a meal in a restaurant or watch a movie or visit a friend's home. Nothing but recovery.

This weekend he not only went to shul, he attended two engagement parties and a barbeque. Although the road ahead is still long with many unknowns, Mel is delighted to be rejoining society!

Please continue to keep Mel in your prayers and mitzvot. Your efforts are truly making a difference. It is clear that Hashem is responding in the affirmative!

Steps

End of Week 16

August 23, 2013

Progress is made in different ways. One way is through gradual development over time coupled with patience and a positive attitude. Much of Mel's improvement can be accounted for in this way. Another way to achieve progress is by seeking answers outside the box and using innovation and determination. This week Mel demonstrated his ability to do the latter method as well.

He was having difficulty climbing steps. His left knee (the stronger at this point) is also the same knee in which Mel had not one but two ACL surgeries prior to the accident. During therapy, he suggested using the right leg to lead up and follow down when working on the stairs. This was the opposite of the way that both PTs assessed the situation. Amazingly, it worked! Mel has since successfully walked up and down our front steps numerous times, the stairs in our house and even steps leading to friends' homes. With just one forearm crutch and a railing, he is good to go. This is incredibly huge, because it enables him access to most homes and buildings!

As we say on Pesach, Dayenu (it would have been enough) for one week, but Mel improved in his walking to such a degree, that it's hard to keep up. He is now walking in and around our home with forearm crutches instead of the walker, and at PT yesterday he practiced walking with only ONE forearm crutch. His gait is smooth, and it is truly remarkable.

Much gratitude every moment to Hashem and to all for your continual prayers and efforts on Mel's behalf.

Please continue to daven and please focus your efforts on increased sensation (the nerves are the slow, gradual development type of progress) and for Mel to be able to continue to improve each and every day.

Shabbat Shalom

Fellow Travelers

The spinal cord injury unit was always busy. Most of the rooms were filled during Mel's months at Kernan, and we got to know his neighbors and therapy-mates.

Barbara's room was just next to Mel's in the far corner of the hallway. Her injury was caused by complications from spinal surgery. A beautiful, quiet woman with short gray hair, a ready smile and a devoted husband, Barbara's days were spent much like Mel's. Her husband and I passed each other in the hall every day, and, without fail, we would exchange updates and progress reports. We shared the bond of the caregiver, and we each put on a brave front to face each demanding day.

The weeks flowed along, and Barbara was making progress. I remember one bright sunny June day on the front lawn by the flagpole that stood in the middle of the hospital's expansive grounds. Mike led the group outside to play the day's game, Toss Across. Barbara's hair shimmered in the sunlight as she raised her arm and threw the ball toward a spot on the lawn, laughing at her good throw. On that day, it struck me that she and Mel were on par with one another; their positioning in the wheelchairs, their fingers curved with tone, yet their arms able to make a decent throw. They were both progressing beautifully, I thought.

As the weeks passed, things began to change. We learned that Barbara had ALS. Not only did she stop making progress, but whatever progress she had made actually reversed. She was discharged at the end of June. Her husband took her home after extensive renovations were made in their home, and a special car was purchased to transport Barbara and her electric wheelchair.

Spotting the couple at a July 4th celebration on Kernan's front lawn, I asked, "How is it to be home?"

"Wonderful," Barbara said.

"We're doing well," her husband added.

I envied them, even though I knew that it was probably not so wonderful and more likely extremely difficult and challenging.

Barbara had several weeks of therapy at home and then she began therapy treatments at Kernan. Mel was also having outpatient therapy by that time. His progress had improved exponentially. He was walking with forearm crutches and moving around the gym on his own. Unfortunately, Barbara's progress had declined at the same rate. She was no longer able to move her arms or legs unassisted, and worse, she could no longer speak. In just a few short months, Barbara lost her battle with ALS and by early fall, she passed away. We remember her warm laughter, her excitement when she told us that her son and daughter-in-law were coming to visit, and that she made it to their wedding.

***

Mel watched with a look of yearning as a large African American man tossed a ball up and down. He was one of the mainstays in Mel's unit. Although his hands looked similar to Mel's, closed and tight, he had found a way to control the ball. Mel's eyes went up and down, following closely. The man smiled when he saw us watching.

I would see him near the front door when I came to the hospital in the morning. He often needed help.

"Will you tie my shoes for me?" he would ask.

"Of course," I would say, putting down my things and bending down to tie them.

"Thanks."

"Glad to help. Have a great day," I smiled back. This routine occurred most week days.

Mel's favorite memory of this fellow patient was watching his escapades in the parking lot. Together with another patient, they often zipped around the lot doing wheelchair wheelies, dust flying as they passed and their hoots filling our ears.

Often I would wonder about the other patients. I noticed that this man did not have a wife or friend as his caregiver, but I do remember his hearty laugh as he carried a young boy on his lap through the hall on the Fourth of July. Smiles lit their faces, and I was relieved to see that he was not alone.

***

Another neighbor was a good-looking young man, possibly in his early twenties, a girlfriend by his side most days. We learned that he was an athlete, a baseball player. We weren't privy to the origin of his injuries, but we witnessed his anger often. An injury of this magnitude can surely and easily erode one's outlook, and it is understandable that one would rail against the injustice. His days at Kernan overlapped with Mel's by a small number. His recovery seemed to be progressing well, and I hope he kept on that trajectory. Before his girlfriend surrendered and abandoned him, I hope he found some peace and acceptance.

Week 27

November 7, 2013

For most of the past six months, Mel has embodied many of the yoga philosophies I teach in my classes. He has stayed in the present using the mind and body that he had on each particular day, working on the tasks at hand with singular attention and commitment and striving to succeed. He used his mind and body in tandem to push himself, yet recognize and honor those limitations, albeit hopeful that the limitations of his body would be temporary.

Baruch Hashem, Mel has been blessed with an incomplete spinal cord injury rather than a complete injury. Although he has had to work with herculean resolve to build strength and develop his muscular movement, progress was and continues to be not only possible but likely, with full functionality an attainable goal.

This week, I spent some quality time speaking with Will, a personable college-aged young man whose time overlapped with Mel's as an inpatient at Kernan. We saw this young man every day, but he did not share his story. This week, as I sat reading in a quiet area of the gym, he approached me in his wheelchair and struck up a conversation. Will's optimism and openness about his situation were profound. He was injured in an automobile accident and was thrown off his motorcycle into a stone wall. His injury is lower than Mel's on the spinal cord, and his injury is complete. Except for his arms and hands, he has no feeling, no movement and no control of anything below his chest. He spoke of treatments outside the U.S. to regain some feeling. He spoke of learning to drive again with hand controls. He spoke of re-evaluating every aspect of his life and how he is handling that. He spoke about wanting to stand — if just for a moment. I listened, I asked questions, and I felt for him with all my being. Although I will be watching and praying for him, he didn't leave me feeling sad because his optimism was palpable.

He shook my hand and wheeled away. I, much the better for the time spent together, looked over at Mel. With incredible Hakarat haTov I watched as Mel sidestepped his way along the floor, concentration furrowing his brow. He is still progressing every day. Baruch Hashem.

Walking and Gait Training

Will he walk again? That was a question many asked and God answered. Yes. But the process was laborious. Mel's PTs worked painstakingly on all the details. Beth built his muscles one by one until he could stand and he could manage a short circuit around the therapy gym. Tasha took over in outpatient therapy and made this miracle a reality.

Mel learned to walk again. Unlike a child who learns by trial and error, falling often, Mel was trained to walk. Falling was not an option, because getting back up was not in the current range of doable activities. Careful preparation and small increments were used as progress was made slowly. Toned muscles limit his range, and minimal sensation on the bottoms of his feet make lifting his foot and placing it down a huge challenge. Thankfully, he has decent proprioception, the ability to sense his foot in space. Not a given under the circumstances.

It took intense concentration, but Mel learned to lift his foot a workable amount to bring it down heel to toe with appropriate force and then bring weight to the moved foot. The mechanics were broken down and mastered. Beth brought a rolling walker with forearm platforms. With it, he walked twenty feet, then forty feet and eventually a short circle around the PT area of the gym. By the time he finished his inpatient therapy, he had progressed to a regular walker.

Tasha proceeded to gait training. She taught him to keep his feet hip distance apart and to keep his foot as he moved it forward from crossing the imaginary midline in front of him. She taught him how to swing his arms – left arm forward as right foot progresses, right arm forward as left foot moves. Many exercises focused on balance, specifically working on transferring weight foot to foot. Quickly, he progressed from walker to two forearm crutches then to one forearm crutch and then to only a cane. For a time, I thought the cane would be a long time necessity, but I was proven wrong. By spring, Mel put the cane aside and walked on without any tool or assistance.

Week 28

November 17, 2013

This was a week of progress marked by the absence and removal of apparatus. With gratitude to Hashem and the gratitude of all those who had made the installation possible, we watched as the chair lifts that were installed with the love and guidance of our dear friends and the amazing chesed of CHAI (a local charitable agency) were removed. This was a big step (pun intended) representing the profound change that has taken place. Mel now handles steps with relative ease, often the one-step one foot method rather than one step two-feet method (landing on one foot and then bringing the other foot up to meet it on the same step before continuing). Mel's comfort and assurance that he no longer needed the lifts and sending them off to serve others is remarkable in such a short time frame and we feel truly blessed. Our home now works for us once again.

Also, this past week, the loaner wheelchair was picked up and taken away. Although the company left the personalized chair that had been ordered, it is relegated to a storage area hopefully never to be used. The removal of the chair from the living room was also a bracha. Mel has not used a wheelchair in weeks and now manages the mile long walk to shul with ease. This past Shabbat he walked approximately two and a half miles at least half of the distance without any helping apparatus (i.e. cane!) His gait was smooth and his balance beautiful to behold. A huge milestone week!

In addition, Mel's strength is improving with each passing day. We needed to weigh a bag, and Mel held it up while I read the weight from the hand-held scale. The display read 40.8 pounds, and Mel managed it without incident! I am constantly amazed at the miracles I see every day. It was only five short months ago that he could barely hold a plastic spoon!

Therapy continues three times a week, and Mel continues to work hard and come home tired from his exertions. A good tired, which thankfully is being rewarded by progress. His stamina is building and he is now able to learn each day.

Please continue to daven on his behalf with an emphasis on hand recovery and functionality.

Shavua Tov to all.

Week 29

November 22, 2013

Mel's new routine continued. Therapy three mornings a week followed by rest and life therapy. The regular activities of daily living should never be trivialized. I often find myself smiling as I notice Mel performing his daily activities with independence. He is often frustrated, because his movements are not as efficient as he expects. I am amazed that he can do them at all! Months ago, I watched as Mel struggled to breathe and then to drink and eat. Those challenges were followed by the painstaking and arduous rebuilding of each muscle in his body with constant prayers that progress would continue without plateau or setback, So far, baruch Hashem, this has been so. Even though there is still much recovery to resume full functionality at a level to which he is content, he is experiencing and appreciating life.

The cadence of this new life is very different than at any other time. Instead of the frantic rhythm of life prior to injury and then the out-of-control staccato of shock trauma and inpatient rehab, the cadence of our life now is rather calm. It is quieter, yet more predictable. Mel's days are filled with praying, therapy and/or exercise, and learning. It is the cadence of healing. With gratitude to Hashem, his pain level remains low and his stamina is increasing exponentially. He is able to attend more functions outside the home (even at night time — which had not been the case). He learns with his regular havruta, attends all his regular shiurim via computer and starting this past week embarked upon a new subject of study with Rabbi Silber a few times a week as well. Thank you to Rabbi Silber for finding the time and bringing such joy to Mel.

The highlight this weekend was Mel realizing a profound accomplishment. Our dear friends Barbara and Howard celebrated the wedding of their oldest daughter. These friends came to visit regularly and with extreme kindness throughout Mel's recovery, and we often discussed the upcoming event. Mel declared in the depths of the summer and amidst the most difficult and unknown time that he would dance at the wedding. And he did! This past motzei Shabbat, broad smiles and camera clicking recorded the moment of wonder as Mel joined those on the dance floor without cane, crutch or wheelchair, danced and swayed to the music for over 20 minutes. Absolutely incredible, miraculous and simply Mel!

Please continue to daven for Mel that he be able to resume more and more of life and return to complete and full functionality in the near future.

Shavua Tov!

Week 30

November 30, 2013

This week we began to celebrate the holiday of Chanukah. On Chanukah, the Festival of Lights, we celebrate the many miracles that Hashem did for us in the time of the Hasmonean revolt and their victory over the mighty Greek army. Hashem's hand was clearly guiding the righteous and leading them to success.

We light eight candles in commemoration of the victory and the fact that the small jar of oil that was found in the desecrated Beit Mikdash lasted for eight nights. It is our custom to light one candle the first night, two the second and so on building up to the eight.

I have taken note and often mentioned the miracles of Mel's recovery, but as I watched him light the candles the past four nights, I was awed anew at the compilation of miracles it has taken to get Mel to the point of recovery he now is.

With wonder, I watched as Mel walked up the steps and over to the menorah with sure footing and no aid (Miracle #1). Then he stood unaided before the Chanukiah (Miracle#2), held the match between his fingers with sensation and dexterity (Miracle #3), bent over the candles with balance (Miracle # 4), intoned the brachot (blessings) with a clear, strong voice (Miracle #5), lit each candle with steady arm and working hand muscles (Miracle #6) and blew

212

out the match with a clear airway and breath that comes from fully functioning lungs (Miracle #7).

As Mel wrapped his arm around me shortly after the lighting, I took note of the eighth and most important miracle of all.

Mel is here beside me. Hashem has and continues to guide him along the path of recovery, His miracles clearly evident!

Happy Chanukah to all.

Week 31 (and 30)

December 10, 2013

Back in May, as Mel was beginning his recovery at Kernan, our daughter, son-in-law and grandson had rushed to be with us, and then had to return to Israel, where they live. When Mel and I said goodbye, our hearts felt leaden because we truly did not know when we would see them again. At that time it was inconceivable that we would be able to make the trip to be with them in the foreseeable future.

Baruch Hashem the miracles of Mel's recovery are boundless, and last night we returned home from a two week visit with our daughter, our son-in-law and our now TWO adorable grandsons! The travel was challenging but Mel managed beautifully. Meeting our new grandson was pure joy and seeing Mel hold him and play with him true bracha.

During our visit, Mel continued to amaze us all. He danced at two weddings, walked great distances over difficult terrain as well as up and down the hills of Jerusalem and Efrat. He managed innumerable steps (97 steps to get to the shul on Shabbat) and Mel climbed and descended them four times over the course of the day alone! He got down on the floor and played with our grandsons, rolling balls, reading books, playing with trains and cars. At the park one day he accomplished his craziest feat of all. He climbed up a seven-rung metal ladder, pulled himself up onto the platform and then slid down a winding tunnel-like slide all for the amusement of our grandson, who wanted Saba to join him. To be honest, I often worried, but Mel is Mel and it is his drive and determination that has gotten him this far on the road to recovery.

The trip was a delight, and we truly are blessed to have had the ability to go. I recently read a story about a spinal cord injured man whose father died. His significant other was trying to figure out a way to get the man to a neighboring state to visit the gravesite of his father, having missed the funeral. There were many challenges to overcome since the man needed full time assistance to manage even the most basic of life functions. The man's recovery does not truly compare to Mel's but the article made me realize anew how fortunate we are. As I watched Mel rest on the long plane rides, I was ever grateful to Hashem for allowing us the opportunity to make the trip and to be with our children and grandchildren – the most important thing in the world!

Shavua Tov to all! Enjoy the winter wonderland. (I hear it is also supposed to snow in Israel this week).

Black Ice

"Are you sure you want to go alone? Do you want me to go with you to the synagogue?" I asked as I helped Mel put on his gloves. Not such an easy or quick task, I had to forcibly straighten each finger and push them into the gloves one by one.

"No. I'll be fine. The ground looks clear." He kissed me goodbye and walked outside, the cold air hitting him in the face. I noticed him shrug deeper into his heavy wool coat before I closed the door.

Months later, Mel told me the real story of his crazy adventure walking to synagogue that icy day. This is what he told me:

I walked carefully, staying in the center of the cul-de-sac and holding my cane in one hand and my tallit bag in the other. Five minutes into my fifteen walk, and I was feeling good, independent, in control. I took a deep breath. Cutting through the Willowbrook Apartments complex, I slowly made my way across the long parking lot. Suddenly, I lost my footing and found myself flat on my back. My cane went flying in one direction, my tallit bag in the other. Stunned, I remained in place long enough to take stock of my body. Everything seemed to be intact. I tried frantically to figure out how I was going to get back on my feet. The ground was coated with black ice and my cane had landed far out of reach. I heard someone from the apartments get into his car. I tried to get his attention as he drove past, believing that he would surely see me and stop and help me up. But he didn't, and drove off. I watched his car and then another car close behind him disappear down the lot.

Slowly and with great difficulty, I turned over onto my stomach. I slid myself along the ground, inching closer and closer to the cars parked on my right. Somehow I managed to retrieve my cane along the way. I needed to find something to support me as I tried to stand up. I reached out and took hold of the closest door handle with my gloved hand. Both the door and handle were covered with ice. Using my cane and the door, I pulled myself up, first to a kneeling and eventually to a standing position, praying all the while that I wouldn't lose my footing or balance.

As I stood up I noticed that my tallit bag was lying on the ground in the middle of the parking lot. To retrieve it or not, that was the question. I allowed myself to take three steps, getting within cane distance of the bag. I figured that if I was still upright, I could reach out with the cane and slide the bag along the ice toward me.

It worked. I bent down, picked up my bag, brushed myself off, and continued on my otherwise successful walk to the synagogue.

Week 32

December 15, 2013

The weeks keep marching on. It is hard to believe that spring turned to summer and then fall and now winter, its unique intensity is upon us. Mel is managing beautifully with the difficult weather. He walked to shul by himself this week stepping carefully along the potentially icy sidewalks, carrying his cane much of the way rather than using it. His stamina is definitely improving. We are able to attend some evening events and are returning to more normal social functioning. Baruch Hashem, we are still seeing progress, although his hands are still a big issue. He has a great deal of tone in the hands, especially the right, dominant one. This means that certain muscles in the hands are very strong, which normally would be a good thing. In this case, the strength of the muscles is prohibiting the movement of the complementary muscles and causing them to be ineffective. Tomorrow he will have a procedure to try to break the tone, temporarily paralyze some of the strong muscles in order to build strength in the weaker muscles. It is our hope that this Botox procedure will speed up the recovery and give him full functionality.

Please daven that the procedure will be successful and that Mel will realize full use of his hands in the near future. Your prayers and kindnesses are appreciated more than you will ever know.

Shavua Tov (A good and successful week to all).

Week 33

December 24, 2013

Mel's procedure last week was relatively pain free, and he is already experiencing some improvement in his right hand. The expected residual effects of the injections should last approximately three months. Mel will be working hard at home and in OT to strengthen his weaker muscles during that time.

This week we decided to return the forearm crutches we had borrowed from a Gemach a local free-loan organization that specializes in medical equipment. When I called the coordinator, she told me that not five minutes prior, someone had called asking for forearm crutches. Unlike wheelchairs, for example, forearm crutches are a more unusual request. The beautiful coordinator explained to me that this happens often, needs are fulfilled within minutes, even unusual or hard to find items. In my new understanding of life and God's world, I was truly touched but not overly surprised. We have seen so many miracles, so many acts of kindness and have been privileged to gain a new understanding of the good that happens all the time. Without delay, I drove to the Gemach and returned the crutches, grateful to be part of this amazing chain of chesed.

Our many thanks to all the wonderful people who help with the Gemachs around the city and please know that your work is appreciated!

Week 34

December 27, 2013

In Mel's words, "this was a slow week." That may be true in the scheme of recovery progress, but not in the scheme of life and a return to normalcy. We attended various social events and Mel showed marked improvement in stamina. We ran errands throughout the week and Mel pushed the carts, carried some of the bags, opened doors for me and did not tire nearly as easily as in past weeks.

I managed to return to work for the first full days since Mel was injured, and Mel managed independently at home and without assistance on outings with friends. On Shabbat, I overslept for the first time since the accident. Mel quietly got himself together, dressed, ate a small breakfast, put on his coat, took his tallit bag and went off to shul without any help from my sleeping self.

When Mel was lying in his hospital bed during his first few days at Shock Trauma, a very special nurse encouraged me by telling me that Mel would function, he would live, and that the extent of that functionality or life was questionable. Only time would tell. And time is telling. The first eight months have been miraculous. Mel is truly reaching independence. I can now oversleep. Baruch Hashem Mel can manage independently.

I don't think it was a "slow" week.

Week 35

January 2, 2014

For weeks and months, caring individuals have stopped me to ask when their favorite pharmacist would be back behind the counter. For many, their relationship with Mel goes back to the years of Shapiro's and Colonial when Mel was building his business. So many beautiful stories have been shared with me; stories of long standing customers who only trust Mel to fill their prescriptions and answer their sensitive questions, stories of the special circumstance where Mel helped them when no one else could, stories of Mel's kindness, understanding and commitment to excellence in his work, but excellence that was always and uniquely filled with heart. He has been proud to serve as the community's pharmacist for nearly 30 years.

To better emphasize my point, Mel received an award from Rite Aid in the mail today. He was recognized as a Rite Aid 2013 Favorite Pharmacy Team Member. The accompanying letter included the following words of thanks signed by the Chairman and CEO as well as the Executive Vice President of the company.

Thank you for realizing our mission every day and for exemplifying greatness in your field. Please know how grateful we are for your expertise, your professionalism and for your unwavering dedication to our customers' individual wellness.

Words that truly do apply to Mel.

Mel's family medical leave ran out in October and Rite Aid did not extend his absence. In order to avoid termination, they asked when he would be able to return to work. Although he is not physically ready to return at full capacity, two weeks ago Mel spoke to his doctor and occupational therapist at Kernan. It was agreed by all that he may be able to handle a very reduced workday and he is willing to try. He contacted the Human Resource department at Rite Aid to apprise them of the new development and to discuss options.

A few hours after Mel received his award and recognition, he heard back from the Human Resource department: The official word was that there are no pharmacist positions available. They are fully staffed. His position has been filled. No accommodations will be made, so Mel will not be returning to Rite Aid to work.

Sometimes change is thrust upon us. What we do with it and how we view it is up to us. It is a new year, and it is time for Mel to truly start anew. It will be a good thing for him to move on, and I know that he will find himself better for it.

Changing the Outcome

I love time travel. The concept simply fascinates me. To go back or forth and experience life in another era would be the ultimate enlightenment. Imagine taking the knowledge and experiences of our own time and comparing it firsthand with those of another era, facing the similarities and differences and coming to fuller realization of the truths of human existence. How huge that would be! I mostly romanticize the possibilities and I believe there would be incredible hardships as well. Mel laughs at me, but I read and watch everything I come across that touches on this fantastic theme.

More than a year after the accident, while flipping through the cable channels, I came across the British time travel movie succinctly titled, *About Time*. I only caught the tail end, maybe the last five minutes, but it was enough for me to want to watch the whole movie. I spent the next several minutes surfing the dial for another chance to watch. Determination won out. I found it listed on the HBO Free movies section. Great, I thought, noting that it was available for the whole next month.

Sunday evening, I found time to watch my time travel movie. I settled in, excited to see it from start to finish. The Fast of Gedalia was winding down and taking its toll on me. Fasting just one day after the Jewish New Year, Rosh Hashana, during which I had eaten my fill, my fast wasn't going very well, and I wasn't feeling my best. Putting all that aside, I sat enchanted as I watched.

The movie's premise was that the main character, a young man, had inherited the ability to travel back in time to any moment within his own life span. By huddling in a dark closet and flexing his fists with intent, he was able to return to past situations and change what happened. Sometimes he had to return again and again to get the right result.

Mel came home with just a half hour to go in the movie. I was needed in my own time, so I turned off the movie and proceeded to deal with our much-needed post-fast eating and drinking.

I wanted to watch the end and put the pieces together. So after work on Monday, I carved out half an hour to finish the movie. Mel joined me.

"In the end, he decided to stop travelling back in time. He decided it was better to live life as it came, to experience it as it was intended without interference," I said, explaining the ending to Mel over dinner. "For a while, he followed his father's advice and repeated days. He would experience the stress and angst that all of us do as we see life unfolding, but then he would go back and redo the day. The second time he was able to find much more enjoyment, knowing that things would work out. Then, he was able to relax even through the difficult moments."

"I wonder what would happen if I did a redo of that morning," Mel said, trailing off.

I looked up at him. Clearly his thoughts were on the day of the bike accident and that life-changing moment of impact.

"You could redo the moments around the accident. You could leave the house a few minutes before or after. That's all it would take to change the outcome," I said.

"Yes. But we don't know if something worse would have happened instead. The past sixteen months would definitely look different. But better for sure?"

"Honey, I don't know. You've been through so much, but you've made it through. I know we would never wish to do it all again, but your journey has certainly given strength to others. Maybe this was the mission that God had for you," I said remembering something I had learned from our rabbi.

The rabbi's topic had been Queen Esther, heroine of the Purim story, during a period in Jewish history when the Jews were threatened with annihilation by the evil Haman. Mordechai, Esther's uncle, told her to go to King Achashverosh and plead for the lives of the Jews of the Persian kingdom who were in mortal danger. Esther hesitated. She told Mordechai that the king had the power to kill her instantly if she approached him without being summoned.

"Do you remember Rabbi S.'s Purim message?" I asked. "This is your time, Mordechai had told Esther. This is your time to act. If you do not act, someone else will, and you may miss the reason you were put on this earth. Perhaps you and your whole family existed for just this one action. If you do not act, you may not fulfill your mission. Someone else will be the vehicle for God's will."

"Yeah. I remember. I don't know. I don't know that anything has really changed for anyone else," he said.

"Well I do," I stated. "People still stop me nearly every day to ask about you and to tell me how your determination and recovery helped them personally to put their own lives and problems in perspective. That's a big deal."

Lapsing into our individual thoughts on the matter, we were quickly startled back to the here and now as the phone rang. Mel got up to answer it. He stood, walked across the floor, lifted the phone from the cradle, and used dexterous fingers to press the talk button. Finally, he took a breath and spoke into the phone.

I recognized the significance in his seemingly ordinary actions. I could *still* see the miracles. I watched him with a huge smile on my face. What a blessing!

Would we choose to change things? I thought. At first blush, the answer was definitely "yes." But the more I thought about it as I watched Mel on the phone, the less sure I was. Would we gamble on a better outcome or would we be thankful for how far we had come? The answer isn't so simple.

Author's Caution: Risking Everything

While waiting at the busy intersection in my silver Nissan Altima for the light to turn green, I watch a cyclist pass me in the opposite direction. I notice it all: Neon yellow shirt, tight bike shorts, black helmet with white lettering, super-thin bike wheels with reflectors. Fully aware that he believes he is doing something positive, something healthy, I reign in my overwhelming desire to yell out the window, "Please get off the roads with that bike. You are risking everything!" As the light changes, I turn away, knowing that I am in the minority; my experiences have shattered my outlook on this "healthy activity," coloring it black and red.

During the nicer weather, it's harder. Almost every day, I pass cyclists moving through and around traffic. I want to embrace them and shake them at the same time. They don't know. Very few actually know what really happens when bike meets car. Intellectually, everyone nods heads and mouths "yes, I know," but they don't.

I do.

"Please get off the roads with that bike. You are risking everything!"

Mel believed that biking was a great form of exercise. With his work and involvement in community causes, he wasn't able to fit too many rides into his busy schedule. I cautioned him nearly every time he rode to be careful, and he was. He did everything right: the clothing, the visibility, he took all the necessary precautions.

That didn't change the outcome.

That didn't change the fact that he needed to fight for his life and rebuild his entire body.

All it took was one bad decision and one second in time to change Mel's life forever, to change our lives forever. It came down to one poor decision, not by my husband but by someone else, someone driving a car, someone who didn't yield the way, someone who needed to get home one second sooner. That same person walked away from the accident, while my husband lay battered on the street with a broken neck.

I make plenty of room for cyclists. My heart speeds up as I pass them. I pray they will make it home safely.

Final Thought

One evening almost three years after the accident, Pam and Neil joined us for dinner at a local restaurant. The noisy sounds of the bustling establishment faded into the background as our little group reminisced.

"How did you keep your focus and optimism?" Neil asked.

After a few thoughtful moments, Mel said, "I never thought recovery wasn't possible. I thought if I worked hard enough, everything would come back."

Stunned by his response, I realized that Mel and I had been working from different vantage points. Mine was kept in check by Karen's warning. I never lost faith that more recovery was possible, but pragmatically, I realized that everything, all recovery, was a far-off dream. I viewed each improvement as a blessed achievement in its own right. The possibility of another achievement was only that, a possibility.

In contrast, Mel viewed each improvement also as an achievement, but one gained through sweat and tears, approved by God. Each achievement was a stepping stone that brought him closer to his ultimate recovery. By following the instructions of his doctors and therapists, keeping his faith and putting forth the effort – at least 200%, more functionality would be attained. He believed that he had the power.

Wow, I thought. I finally get it. Along with the fact that Mel's injury to his spinal cord was incomplete and some degree of recovery was possible, the key to Mel's amazing progress was rooted in his mental fortitude. With faith and empowerment, everything had been possible. For Mel, it made all the difference. It kept him fighting. It kept him focused. Dr. Y., a specialist in spinal cord injury at Kernan and Mel's primary doctor, once told Mel that he was on par with his most recovered patient. He had been doing this type of work for over seven years at the time.

"Your progress is off the charts," he told Mel.

Although Mel did not achieve a complete and total return to normal functioning or sensation, he has come pretty damn far. Challenges definitely remain, yet he fought an amazing battle. I proudly proclaim him the victor!

Epilogue

MEL

"I'll be ready in a minute," Judy said.

"Take your time," I called back as I walked out the door of our upstairs bedroom. Making my way down the two short set of steps, I passed our temporary abode as Judy called it, now back to guest bedroom status. I pulled out my cell as I reached the main floor and found the stopwatch app.

I headed out to the front porch and sat in the nearest chair. The sun was strong, and I put on my sunglasses. Bending down, I tightened the shoe laces on my walking shoes. Everything I do using my fingers takes real effort but I persevere.

"Let's go," I said as Judy came out the front door.

I followed her down the front steps and we headed toward the street.

"Our regular route?" she asked.

"Sure," I responded as I started the stopwatch. I knew that it would take about an hour to walk the two-and-a-half-mile circuit that we like to make around the neighborhood, but it is part of my competitive nature that I need to know exactly how quickly we make each trip. That hasn't changed.

Carefully putting the cell in the pocket of my basketball shorts, I focused on each step as we walked along, making sure my legs didn't drag, careful not to veer too far right or left. I must concentrate. The numbness in my legs and the lack of sensation in my feet continues to make walking challenging. I don't feel the ground below me nearly as much as before the accident.

"It's a nice day," Judy said. "I think five degrees cooler would be perfect."

"It seems fine to me," I said, not really sure. My internal thermometer is still out of whack. Before the accident, I would already be sweating from the heat, dripping by the time I would finish a run or a ride. Now I don't feel it so much, and I only sweat on intense exertion.

As we passed the high school, I glanced at the tennis and basketball courts. I tried not to focus on the disappointing reality that my playing days are over. In many ways, I was defined by my abilities to play these sports. Although now I am relegated to spectator status, I still pull from the many life lessons learned on the courts.

Just as we turned left onto Labyrinth Road, I briefly looked straight down Smith Avenue a short block ahead to the intersection of Carla Road, the site of the accident. Shaking my head, I focused my thoughts and attention on moving forward.

"I spoke to Shana this morning. Did you know that the babies are already trying to roll over? They're so adorable," Judy said.

"She told me yesterday. Yonatan is almost able to do it, but cute babbling-brook Tehilla is just starting to try." As I answer, I picture our newest grandchildren, born just three months ago. I feel incredibly fortunate that we were able to travel to Israel to be with them after the births, like healthy people, traveling without the wheelchairs, walkers, and assistance at the airports that were necessary on our first trip post-accident. Although my adventures at the airports took significantly longer than in my previous life, I saw real progress in my recovery as I managed without incident. I smile as I remember meeting the twins, playing with their big brothers, and holding Yonatan at his *brit milah*.

"Life is good," I said summing up my thoughts.

"Yes, it sure is," she smiled looking my way.

As we turned left and began the trek up Clark's Lane, the last incline of our walk, I was eager to see if I could keep my pace. Up the 0.6 mile hill we went. I knew that I was working very hard when a single bead of sweat dropped from my brow.

As we turned toward home, I noticed Judy watching me as always, and I realized anew how blessed I have been and continue to be to have her by my side throughout this life-changing ordeal.

Back on our front porch, I checked my stopwatch and smiled at the time, a bit quicker than the last. Judy gave me the thumbs up as she went into the house.

I stood on the porch staring ahead but focused inward. The realities of my new life are often glaring and difficult. I recognize and understand that I now have physical limitations that I must contend with each and every day. That doesn't deter me. I want to be there for my wife, my children, my grandchildren, my friends and my community, so I will face each day going forward with the same positive outlook and drive that has brought me from the despair of those first days at Shock Trauma, through the gut-wrenching work of recovery, and to this different yet purposeful life.

Made in the USA
Columbia, SC
25 April 2018